Luke

A CONTEXTUAL APPROACH
to Bible Study

by
Paul Germond

COLLINS

Collins Liturgical Publications
8 Grafton Street, London W1X 3LA

Harper & Row
Icehouse One — 401
151 Union Street, San Francisco, CA 94111-1299

Collins Liturgical in Canada
Novalis, Box 9700, Terminal
375 Rideau St, Ottawa, Ontario K1G 4B4

Distributed in Ireland by
Educational Company of Ireland
21 Talbot Street, Dublin 1

Collins Dove
PO Box 316, Blackburn, Victoria 3130

Collins Liturgical New Zealand
PO Box 1, Auckland

ISBN 0 00 599975 8
© 1987 text Paul Germond, illustrations Wm Collins
First published 1988

All scripture quotations are from the *Holy Bible, New International Version*.
Copyright © 1973, 1978, 1984 by International Bible Society. Used by permission.

The two poems 'Two Songs of Elizabeth'
and 'Mary' are © Kathryn Poethig
and used with her permission.

Cover illustration by Sydney Holo
Cover design by Malcolm Harvey Young
Typographical design by Colin Reed
Typeset by Swains (Glasgow) Limited
Made and printed in Great Britain
by Collins, Glasgow

Library of Congress Cataloguing-in-Publication Data

Germond. Paul.
    Portraits of Jesus : Luke

    1. Jesus Christ—History of doctrines—Early church,
ca. 36—600.   2. Bible. N.T. Luke—Criticism,
interpretation, etc.   3. Bible. N.T. Luke—Study.
I. Bible. N.T. Luke. II. Title.
BT198.W67 1988   266'.506   87—18290
ISBN 0-00-599975-8 (pbk.)

Contents

Preface — 5
General Introduction: The Four Portraits of Jesus — 7

INTRODUCTION: FRAMING THE PORTRAIT — 9
Three horizons
    The first horizon: Palestine in the time of Jesus — 10
    The second horizon: Luke's world —
      Greek and Roman — 17
    The third horizon: The Church today —
      Cape Town, South Africa — 18

LUKE'S PORTRAIT OF JESUS — 23
Jesus, the Saviour of the World

BIBLE STUDIES
Who brings God's Salvation?
1 Jesus the Saviour Brings God's Salvation
   (Luke 2:11, 28-32) — 25

Where is God's Salvation to be Found?
2 God's Salvation is Found in Political History
   (Luke 1:5-7, 2:1-6, 3:1-2) — 29
3 God's Salvation is Found in Human Experience
   (Luke 1:5-7, 2:1-6, 3:1-2) — 36
4 Jesus' Manifesto of Salvation (Luke 4:14-30) — 39

Jesus' Salvation Comes in Power and Weakness
5 The Holy Spirit Empowers Jesus' Salvation
   (1:34, 35; 2:25-28; 3:21, 22; 4:1, 2, 14, 18,
   31-37; 12:11, 12) — 45
6 Prayer: the Human Cry for Deliverance
   (Luke 22:39-44; 18:1-8) — 49

Jesus' Salvation in Human Experience

7 Elizabeth: a Woman's Story of Salvation
(Luke 1:5-7, 23-25, 57-58)   55

8 Mary: a Woman's Story of Salvation
(Luke 1:26-56; 2:4-7)   60

9 The Rich Ruler: is Jesus' Salvation too Costly?
(Luke 18:18-30)   64

10 Zacchaeus: Jesus' Salvation is Not too Costly!
(Luke 19:1-10)   69

Jerusalem: The Destiny of God's Salvation

11 Jerusalem: Jesus Journeys to his Destiny
(Luke 9:30-31, 51, 52, 56; 13:22, 31-35; 17:11, 18:31-33; 19:1, 11, 28, 29, 41)   76

12 Jerusalem: Jesus' Salvation in Conflict with the Powerful (Luke 19:45 ... 23:25)   82

13 Jerusalem: Witness to the Risen Saviour
(Luke 24:36-53, Acts 1:8)   92

A Scholarly Note   95
Suggested Readings   96

Preface

This study of the Gospel of Luke emerges from a series of Bible studies at St Philip's Anglican Church, St John's Parish, Wynberg, Cape Town, in July to September 1986. It represents the fusion of my own academic studies with the experience, insights and praxis of the people who make up the congregation of St Philip's. It is to these people and the life of this congregation that I dedicate this book.

Throughout the period in which this book was conceived and written, South Africa was in a state of acute turmoil. The suffering of the oppressed people of this land will never be fully expressed, but I pray that through their struggle the liberation which Christ brings will be shown to a world which knows so little of life in all its fullness.

Kathryn Poethig deserves my special thanks for writing two poems for this book: 'Two Songs of Elizabeth' and 'Mary'; as well as for her most helpful suggestions. To Susan for her enthusiasm for this project and her most practical assistance goes my love and gratitude.

Paul Germond
New York City, December 1987

Jesus
I see you betrayed
by your disciples:
only your enemies
remain what they were.

General Introduction

This study is part of a series of commentaries on the four gospels. The aim of the series is to present the distinct portrait of Jesus which each gospel provides, and yet to do so in a way which shows how the four portraits relate to and complement each other. None of the volumes is therefore intended to be a comprehensive commentary on a particular gospel. The passages chosen for study and reflection have been selected because they portray most vividly the portrait which the evangelist wishes to paint. Yet, when all four volumes are taken as a whole, it will be seen that they cover a great deal of the material found in the four gospels.

The origin of the series is important for understanding what has been attempted. Each of the four authors is a biblical scholar well versed in the contemporary discussion on the gospels. In particular, each has a special interest in the sociology of the New Testament and a contextual approach to Christian faith and theology. Even though much scholarly work lies behind each volume, the authors have not sought to engage in scholarly debate. They have provided, rather, commentaries for use in Bible study groups and by people at the 'grass-roots'. Indeed, the commentaries originated as much within such groups as they did within the scholar's study. For several months each author met with various Bible study groups comprised of people from different denominational, racial and socio-economic backgrounds. Together they explored the gospels in order to discern who Jesus really is for us today. Hence the attempt to locate the portrait of Jesus in three contexts or horizons: his own context; the context of the original evangelist and those to whom the gospel was written; and our own situation today. Each of these is pertinent to understanding who Jesus is for us, and they also provide a way into the study of the gospels which has already proved useful in Bible study groups.

The authors have worked as a team, and each of the four volumes follow a similar pattern. All have used the New International Version of the Bible, and, as already indicated, a premium has been placed by all on a sociological approach to the text. Each volume also contains suggestions as to how they can best be used. There is, therefore, a basic structure common to all four volumes. Yet each author has brought to the task different insights and experiences, gained, not least, from discussing the gospels with people who are struggling in different contexts to be faithful to Jesus Christ in South Africa. This, rather than some rigid formula, has shaped the final product. It is our hope that other Bible study groups will find them of value and use for their own journey of faith and obedience within their particular historical and social context. Our overriding concern is that each person discover the Jesus to whom the four evangelists bear witness.

John W. de Gruchy
Bill Domeris
General Editors

Introduction: Framing the Portrait

Three Horizons

Jesus has been and continues to be one of the most studied figures in human history. Among the earliest books ever written about Jesus are the four books, now called the Gospels, which form the first part of the New Testament: Matthew, Mark, Luke and John. Each Gospel has a different portrait of Jesus for each reflects the unique experience of its author. The authors differed in terms of the place from which they wrote, the audience to whom they wrote, and the reasons for which they wrote their Gospel.

The purpose of this short book is to uncover the unique picture of Jesus which is presented by the writer of the Gospel of Luke. The central questions which will be asked throughout are: 'What was Luke's portrait of Jesus? How did Luke understand Jesus' mission in the world? What does Luke want us to believe about Jesus?' By asking these questions we will be able to discover what makes Luke's Gospel different from the other three Gospels.

If four artists were to paint a portrait of the same person, their final products would all be pictures of the same person but they would undoubtedly be different. One might have painted the face in profile; another, the face with a smile; another, the face fierce and angry; and the fourth, with a background filled with images from that person's life. Each would be different, each stressing different qualities and characteristics of the one person, and at the same time reflecting the particular understanding each artist had of their subject. So it is with the writers of the four Gospels.

As we begin to study the Gospel of Luke we need to be aware of the frame in which Luke's portrait of Jesus is set. Because we are not dealing with a painting hanging on a wall we can expect the frames of Luke's portrait to be more complex and important for our understanding of the portrait. There are three frames (or horizons) which frame Luke's portrait of Jesus, each of which needs our careful attention.

10   The first horizon: Palestine in the time of Jesus

The *first* horizon is the context in which Jesus lived and died. The portrait of Jesus must be set in its specific frame of first century Palestine if we are to begin to understand who Jesus was and how Luke portrays him.

The *second* horizon is the context in which Luke himself lived and wrote. Here it is important to ask questions such as, 'Why did Luke write about Jesus as he did?' and 'To whom was Luke writing, and why was he writing to them?' This frames the actual activity of Luke in a particular context and enables us to better understand Luke's portrait of Jesus.

The *third* horizon is the context in which we live today, in the closing decades of the twentieth century. This context shapes our understanding of Luke's portrait and our ability to apply it in a significant way to our lives and our situation. In this book, South Africa in 1986 and 1987 is the third frame.

This means that there are at all times three points of focus in this book: Jesus in his historical context, Luke in his context and us in our context. The most important underlying assumption in this book is that contemporary human experience is a most important key to understanding the Bible. A constant dialogue between our experience and the text will be established in the studies which follow.

The first horizon: Palestine in the time of Jesus

Jesus was a human being. Like any of us he was born of a mother, suckled at her breast, dirtied his nappies, woke his parents with his crying. He was a toddler, hesitantly learning to walk. He ran around with the other children of the village, unhappy when he had to come in and wash before the evening meal which brought the fun and games of the day to an end. He had to go to school, where he learnt to read the Law and the Prophets in Hebrew. He too grew up and became an adult. The disciples first encountered Jesus as a person, like one of them. Only later in their experience did they come to understand him as the Son of God.

Jesus lived in Nazareth, a village in Galilee, at a time when the Romans were the colonial overlords of Palestine. Like our lives his life must be understood in terms of the context in which he lived. Just as it would be absurd for anyone to try to understand your life as if you lived in a vacuum, so it is absurd for us to try and understand Jesus without understanding him in his environment.

In order to do this we need to look at at least three elements of life in Palestine in the first century: economic life, political life and religious life. These three elements are all closely intertwined but it will help us to try and identify them separately. But first some comments about the geography of Palestine; for understanding its geography will be an important element in our study of the Gospel of Luke.

The geography of Palestine

Palestine in Jesus' time was made up of a number of different Roman territories, the two most important in Jesus' life being Galilee and Judea (see the map on page 12). Galilee was in the North and Judea was in the South and the two were separated by the territory called Samaria. Jesus lived most of his life in Nazareth in Galilee. It was here that he was baptised, called his disciples and began his public ministry. Galilee must for these reasons come under our scrutiny. According to Luke, Jerusalem, the capital of Judea, was the place to which Jesus travelled in order to challenge the dominance of the Jewish elite over the lives of the people of Judea and Galilee. Jesus lived his last days in Judea and was put to death in Jerusalem by the Judean ruling class. Judea and its capital Jerusalem require our consideration as well.

Judea was a small, arid, rocky plateau, surrounded on three sides by natural boundaries which isolated it from the rest of Palestine — of which it formed the southernmost point. Its southern border was the Negeb desert, while to the East lay the deep, hostile rift valley of the Jordan and the saline Dead Sea. Its western border was a series of steep tortuous valleys which marked the edge of the mountain range which ran like a spine down Palestine. The Judean plateau consisted of stony hill country with occasional fertile stretches and little agricultural potential. The villages and towns of Judea lived a precarious existence on this plateau. It was an isolated part of the world, cut off by its natural boundaries. No trade routes crossed Judea. This isolation resulted in a spirit of fierce resistance to foreign influence and a strong sense of national pride. Judea was Jewish through and through. It had no significant gentile population to speak of, apart from the presence of the Roman army and colonial officers.

12 The first horizon: Palestine in the time of Jesus

In contrast, *Galilee* formed the northern extreme of Palestine; bounded in the North by the mountains of Lebanon, in the East by the river Jordan and the Sea of Galilee, and in the West by the coastal

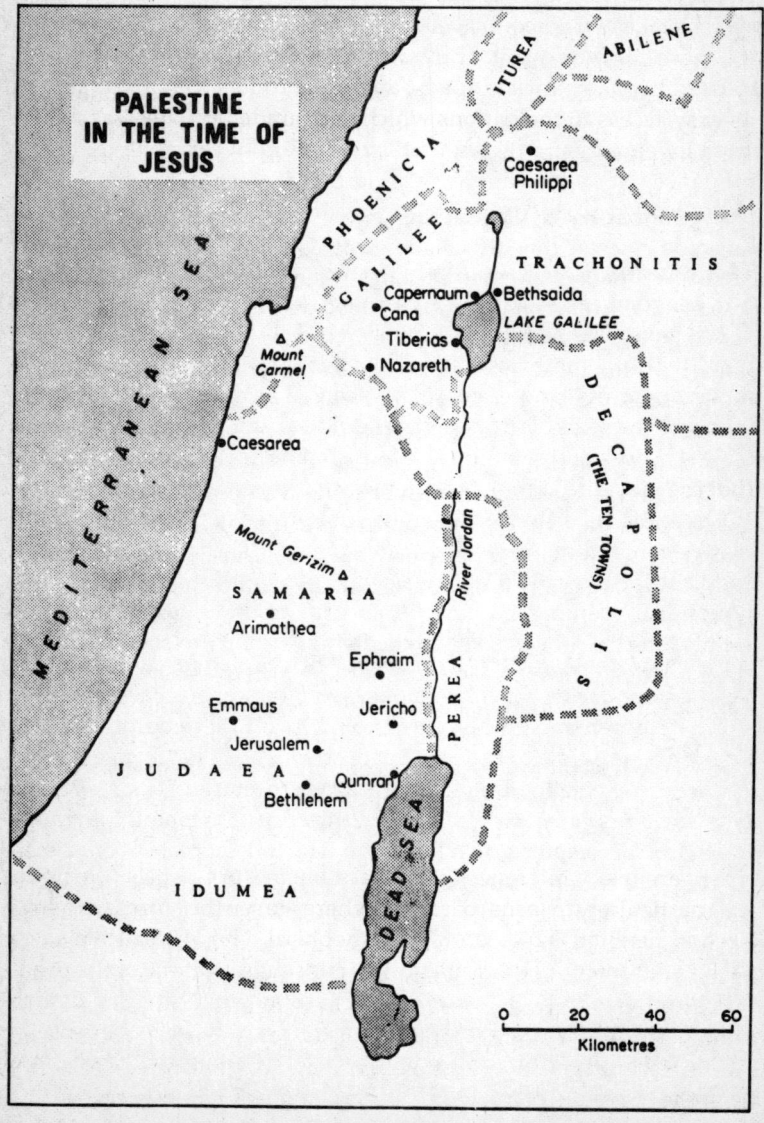

plain. As the highest and most northerly region of Palestine it was the coolest and most lush of them all. Dotted with small villages — with their inevitable olive groves, vineyards and orchards — Galilee was a fertile territory. It was well watered with a number of rivers and the lake of Galilee, as well as a dependable annual rainfall. Galilee, with its fertile soil, was ideal agricultural land. It was crisscrossed by many ancient roads, and trade routes were facilitated by its easy access to the nations which surrounded it. This was no isolated Judea; rather a region that lay open and welcoming to foreign influence. Not surprisingly, we find that Galilee had a large Greek speaking population and that its largest cities were Gentile.

The economy of Palestine in the time of Jesus

The economy in Palestine rested, as it had done for thousands of years, upon the agricultural activity of the village peasantry. The majority of the native Galileans and Judeans lived in small villages and worked the land which they received as their inheritance. The land was the basis of their ability to produce what they needed to stay alive. The loss of this land was a tragedy for the peasants, as it meant that they lost the ability to maintain an independent productive life. Without the subsistence which the land provided the peasant family was dependent on wage labour for survival. The real offence of the prodigal son (Luke 15:11-31) was that he squandered the inheritance which had been passed down from generation to generation in his family, and thereby weakened the family's ability to survive despite their relative affluence. The account of Naboth's vineyard (1 Kings 21:1-28) gives us an indication of how ancient the concept of inheritance was in Israel and how important a role it played in Israelite life. The theological rationale for this economic system of inheritance was that God himself had given the land to his people, and it was therefore to be passed down from generation to generation.

There are many references to peasant life in the Gospels. We notice this particularly in Jesus' parables, where we see the sower who sows seed in his field (Luke 8:5-8), the shepherd who has lost his sheep (Luke 15:3-6), the well-off peasant family in the parable of the prodigal son (Luke 15:11-32) and the vineyard at the centre of a dispute (Luke 20:9-19). These illustrations were used by Jesus because he spent most of his life and public ministry among the peasants of Galilee.

14 The first horizon: Palestine in the time of Jesus

This picture of the peasantry is on the whole common to both Galilee and Judea. But Galilee has an additional feature which is not shared by Judea and which is important to Jesus' background: the sea of Galilee or Gennesaret. The sea of Galilee gave the Galilean peasants a significant alternative in their lifestyle and means of subsistence — fishing. The fishermen of Galilee and the sea upon which they made their living play an important part in the early period of Jesus' work. Jesus calls disciples from their nets (Luke 5:1-11), he teaches from fishing boats (Luke 5:3), he calms a storm on the sea (Luke 8:22-25) and he multiplies two fish from the sea of Galilee in order to feed thousands (Luke 9:10-17).

The peasantry of Palestine lived in small villages with the extended family or household as the primary social unit. These villages were largely self-sufficient. The agricultural activity of their members (plus fishing in Galilee) provided the basic food requirements, while local artisans manufactured what elementary products they required. Jesus' father, Joseph, was one such village artisan, a carpenter (Matthew 13:55), a trade which Jesus himself practised (Mark 6:3). Anything else the villagers needed was procured through barter trade with neighbouring villages. The villages needed very little of what was produced by the cities, whereas the cities were almost entirely dependent on the produce of the villages for their survival.

The other primary agricultural activity in Palestine took place on the large estate farms which were owned, on the whole, by wealthy landlords resident in the cities. The rich fool in Jesus' parable (Luke 12:13-21) is just such a large landowner, and the rich man at whose gate Lazarus begs (Luke 16:19-31) might well have derived his wealth from farms he owned. Generally, the land such people owned had previously been held by the peasants.

Peasants lost their land in a number of ways, the most common of which was debt. Debt was usually incurred by failure to pay taxes. The peasantry of Palestine was severely taxed by a triple taxation: the Roman tax, the temple tax, and the local priestly and synagogue tax. When they were unable to pay their taxes the peasants often had to sell their land, invariably to wealthy land owners. Alternatively, the land was confiscated. One of the most profound effects of the Roman taxation system was that it demanded payment of taxes in cash, which forced the farmers into trading for money on the open market, as opposed to the traditional system of barter. Peasants also lost their land because of the ravages of war or famine. And, particularly in Judea, the very strict religious laws of purity — which defined one's ability to be securely involved in society — often denied people the right to work, for example, the leper (Luke 5:12-16). These outcasts from society barely managed to eke out an existence on the fringes of the cities and villages.

The peasants who were displaced from their land could find employment in a variety of ways. They could rent land from a large land owner and work it themselves as tenant farmers (Luke 20:9-19), or they could become wage labourers on large estates (Matthew 25:33-41). Another possibility was to become an administrator or servant in a wealthy household (Luke 16:1-8). Many would have had to go into the cities to find work. Here they might have found employment on various building projects — Herod the Great's rebuilding of the temple in Jerusalem alone is reputed to have employed 18,000 labourers for forty years. In Galilee, peasants were known to sell themselves into slavery to cover their debts. Women who lost their independent economic base were often forced to resort to prostitution in order to stay alive; this was particularly likely in the Greek cities and towns of Galilee where prostitution was more socially acceptable than in the Jewish towns of Galilee and Judea. Jesus encounters a woman who might well have been a prostitute in a town in Galilee (Luke 7:36-50).

The politics of Palestine in the time of Jesus

Palestine was ruled as a single unit under Herod the Great (47-4 BCE), who was the king over Palestine at the time of Jesus' birth (Matthew 2:1-12). On his death this territory was divided up amongst his sons by the Roman emperor Caesar Augustus. Galilee was given to Herod Antipas which meant that Jesus, for the duration of his adult life, lived under Antipas' political authority. It was this Herod who had John the Baptist beheaded and to whom Jesus was sent, by Pilate, after his arrest because he was a Galilean (Luke 23:6-12). Judea was given to Antipas' brother, Archaelaus. He was not successful at his job of governing turbulent Judea and was replaced by a Roman Procurator in 6 CE. Pontius Pilate was Procurator of Judea when Jesus was crucified.

Although Judea was governed directly by a Roman official, day-today affairs were the responsibility of the Jewish *Sanhedrin*. This had seventy-one members, presided over by the high priest. Although the Sanhedrin's political power was restricted to Judea, its religious authority covered Jews all over the world. Luke loosely characterised this group as 'the chief priests, the teachers of the law and the leaders among the people' (Luke 19:47) and they are portrayed by him as Jesus' primary enemy. He lays responsibility for Jesus' death clearly at their feet, even though, under Roman rule, the Sanhedrin did not have the authority to condemn a person to death. For Luke, the political and religious leaders of Judea were constantly trying to find a way to kill Jesus, because he posed a serious threat to them (Luke 19:47;20:19-20; 22:2).

The religious situation in Palestine in the time of Jesus

The dominant religious feature of Palestine was the *temple in Jerusalem*. Pilgrims from all over the Roman empire flocked to Jerusalem to celebrate the major Jewish festivals at the temple. It symbolised Israel's election as God's chosen people, and was the place at which the Jews most sacred religious ceremonies took place. The temple plays an important part in Luke's account of Jesus' life, particularly in the stories about the birth of John the Baptist and of Jesus. John the Baptist's father, Zechariah, a priest, was serving in the temple when he had a vision of his son's birth (Luke 1:5-25). Jesus was taken to the temple as an infant where Simeon and Anna predicted great things of him (Luke 2:21-38), and as a twelve year-old Jesus accompanied his parents to Jerusalem to celebrate the Passover with them at the temple, which, says Luke, was their custom (Luke 2:41-51).

In Jerusalem, the dominant religious grouping was the *Sadducee* party. The Sadducees enjoyed wealth and power, their wealth coming from the large estates they owned. They were the dominant force in the Sanhedrin. Politically conservative, they collaborated with the Roman authorities who in turn temporarily ensured their positions of privilege.

If Jerusalem was the domain of the Sadducees then the countryside was the domain of the *Pharisees*. A political and religious party, the Pharisees were lay people who responded to the cultural and religious threat of Greek and Roman culture and religion by developing a detailed programme of life, based on the Torah and scribal interpretations, that preserved the distinctiveness of a Jew no matter what the circumstances. The Pharisees established closely bonded groups which met for prayer, study and meals on the Friday before the Sabbath. Highly religious, they were strictly legalistic in their interpretation of the Jewish law. With their power base in the rural areas they had the interests of the villagers at heart.

While Jesus was highly critical of both the Sadducees and the Pharisees, he encountered them in different circumstances: the Pharisees in his work in the country areas, and the Sadducees in the closing months of his life in Jerusalem.

The second horizon: Luke's world — Greek and Roman

Christian tradition and modern scholarship generally agree that the person Luke was the author of both the Gospel of Luke and the Acts of the Apostles. But in fact we know very little about who Luke was and under what circumstances he wrote his account of Jesus and the beginnings of the Christian Church. From his writings we can tell that he was a Gentile Christian, well-educated and able to write good Greek, with a thorough knowledge of the Septuagint (the Greek translation of the Hebrew Bible). There is some debate as to whether Luke, the author of the Gospel and Acts, should be identified with the Luke who is mentioned as the companion of the Apostle Paul in 2 Timothy 4:11. If he was Paul's companion, as I will assume he was and as tradition suggests, he was a doctor, most probably a citizen of Antioch — one of the largest cities of the ancient world.

Luke probably wrote his Gospel between 80 and 90 CE, some forty or so years after the death and resurrection of Jesus. From the Acts of the Apostles we are able to infer that Luke was a companion of Paul from about 40 CE to the time of Paul's death in 65 CE. Luke was not an eyewitness to Jesus' life. His Gospel therefore relies on the accounts of eyewitnesses and on the traditions about Jesus preserved in the Church. Like Matthew, he used the Gospel of Mark extensively. Writing to Theophilus, the person to whom he addressed his works, Luke states that:

> Therefore, since I have fully investigated everything from the beginning, it seemed good also to me to write an orderly account for you, most excellent Theophilus, so that you may know the cer-

tainty of the things that you have been taught. (Luke 1:3-4. See also Acts 1:1)

When Luke wrote his Gospel the Christian Church was at a critical stage in its development. Most of the original apostles and Paul, the great missionary to the Gentiles, had died. The need clearly to state and preserve the traditions about Jesus' life was acute. As part of this general need, Luke wrote his Gospel; a collection of stories, liturgies and traditions which had been passed down verbally and in writing in the context of the worship and life of the various Christian communities scattered around the Roman world.

Further, the Church had bridged its Jewish boundaries, particularly under the influence of Paul, and had become predominantly a Gentile, or more accurately, a Hellenistic Church. This meant that the Church had lost its early Jewish identity and had taken on culturally and philosophically the characteristics of Hellenism — the product of the integration of classical Greek culture with the culture of other Mediterranean societies. The world in which Luke lived would have been culturally Hellenistic, with Greek as the common language, but politically and economically dominated by the Roman empire. Luke wrote his Gospel in such a way as to appeal to people of the Hellenistic world, and to portray Christianity as a reasonable religion to the Roman authorities.

Jerusalem was destroyed by the Romans in 70 CE. When Luke wrote his Gospel the temple no longer existed, the Sanhedrin was disbanded and the chief priests and Sadducees scattered. This meant that Luke could portray the Jewish ruling class in a very negative light without fear of reprisals. The link between the Gentile churches and Jerusalem was becoming increasingly weak, as other Roman and Hellenistic centres became more important.

The third horizon: the Church today — Cape Town, South Africa

Anyone who wishes to read and understand the Bible today must take their contemporary context seriously for at least two reasons. Firstly, because our beliefs, experiences, and values determine to a very large extent our understanding of the biblical text. Secondly, because the Bible must speak to us today in our concrete human

The third horizon: the Church today 19

experience. Therefore, the third horizon of this study — our contemporary experience — is crucial. Cape Town, South Africa, is the concrete reality out of which this study of Luke's portrait of Jesus emerged.

Cape Town is a remarkably beautiful city which nestles at the foot of Table Mountain on the southern tip of Africa. Many people regard it as the most desirable city in South Africa to live in. The physical beauty of the place is awesome. Mountains plunge steeply into the sea, and the many folds in the coastline create an abundance of scenic bays and harbours. Miles of white beaches border both sides of the peninsula, which is renowned for its indigenous flora. Across the Cape flats forty kilometres to the East lie the encircling arms of the Boland mountains, whose valleys are filled with vineyards, oak trees and white Cape Dutch style homesteads. The climate is temperate with long lazy summer days that end in glorious sunsets over the Atlantic Ocean.

It is a sporting paradise. Surfing, boardsailing, fishing, sailing — watersports of all descriptions — hiking, rock climbing in the mountains. Cricket dominates in the summer and rugby in the winter. Cape Town is well known for its scenic marathon races. Educationally it has much to offer. Schools with some of the proudest traditions in the country are linked to the Universities of Cape Town and Stellenbosch. Theatres, cinemas, art galleries, museums, symphony concerts, ballet and fascinating restaurants satisfy the cultural needs of the city's inhabitants.

The residential areas of Bishops Court and Constantia are famous for their gracious homes and beautiful gardens, while Clifton and Camps Bay are the watering spots of the jet set.

All this and so much more is available to you in Cape Town; if you are white and if you are well off.

For there is another Cape Town. The Cape Town of the squatter camps where people live huddled beneath rudimentary plastic shelters in the bitter winter rains. The Cape Town of the single-sex hostels where it is illegal to be joined by one's family, which are empty before the sun rises and are filled after dark by bone-weary workers. The Cape Town of Mitchells Plain, Mannenberg, Atlantis populated by people forcibly removed from their homes and dumped in out-of-

20 The third horizon: the Church today

the-way places to make way for the privileged whites. The Cape Town of vagrant children sniffing glue and drinking methylated spirits in the alleys of the city centre. The Cape Town of apartheid with segregated residential areas, segregated schools and colleges, segregated trains and toilets and segregated lives. The Cape Town of the national state of emergency proclaimed by the Nationalist Party where prisons are filled with thousands of men, women and children detained without trail or recourse to the normal legal process. The Cape Town where it is illegal to burn candles in the streets in protest at the emergency, where it is illegal to call for the release of detained children and political leaders. The Cape Town where thousands of school children live in fear of police raids on their schools; and where hundreds of children were shot and many killed in 1986. The Cape Town where the police and army join forces to occupy the black townships; where to be a policeman or soldier is to be a traitor. The Cape Town where tens of thousands of squatters were rendered homeless by state-backed violence. The Cape Town where churches are harassed and persecuted by the police as they shelter the homeless in their halls. The Cape Town where funerals for community heroes are banned and stopped with violence. The Cape Town on whose TV screens falsehood is truth and truth is falsehood. The Cape Town of the white controlled Parliament which secures the interests of its constituency with ever increasing repressive measures — the Cape Town of oppression, of suffering, of injustice and of violence.

Cape Town is a divided city. Divided between oppressor and oppressed. The divisions are becoming sharper as the months pass.

In this divided country, in this divided city, is the Anglican church of St Philip's, Wetton. This congregation provides the lens through which we will look at Luke's portrait of Jesus. The studies which follow were first done at St Philip's, so the experiences, reflections and insights of its members pervade this book and determine many of the questions and answers in what follows.

St Philip's is the smallest of five congregations which comprise the Parish of St John's. In a well attended service the small church building will be filled by eighty to ninety people. The buildings of the church are located next to a railway line which demarcates a legal boundary between white residential areas and so-called 'coloured' residential areas. The congregation of St Philip's reflects this divide, with people coming from both sides of the line. The life of the congregation has been profoundly affected by this division, with the leadership of the congregation often being disproportionately dominated by whites. Social interaction between the two parts of the congregation outside of church activities is constantly inhibited by the racial climate of South Africa.

In the past year much of this has begun to change, with the leadership of the church moving increasingly into the hands of the politically disenfranchised and a new sense of community emerging in the congregation. A fresh understanding of the role of the Church in the political struggles of South Africa has developed as many of the congregation have increasingly experienced the brutal force of oppression in their lives. Families have had members detained or imprisoned for political reasons. Many of the members of St Philip's are teachers in black schools. They and their pupils have seen police and army forces violently invade their schools — killing and injuring and detaining thousands of pupils and their teachers. Despair, frustration and anger have been dominant moods among these people. The movement towards a greater integration of political struggle and church life has been eventful for St Philip's: some people have left the church in protest at such an integration while others have been highly critical of what they see as an inadequate response, by the congregation, to the crisis the country faces.

St Philip's straddles the two worlds of Cape Town; but does this in an unusual way. Generally the white members of the congregation are from the lower income levels in the white spectrum; while the black members are mainly from the middle to higher income levels in the 'coloured' spectrum. Sociologically both these groups occupy a fairly vulnerable and therefore insecure position in South African society. Lower income whites constantly face the threat of upwardly mobile blacks; and upwardly mobile blacks are often reluctant to do anything that threatens their hard-earned status. These dynamics were part of the complex reactions of the congregation to the crisis that South Africa is going through, and to working out what it means to be a Christian in such a situation.

In this context it was inevitable that the studies on the Gospel of Luke, which resulted in this book, would be profoundly affected by the immediate political situation. At all times we attempted to make

22 The third horizon: the Church today

our experience of life the vantage point from which we approached the text. We consciously used our human experience as the lens through which we examined the Gospel of Luke. But we also wanted the text to speak to our lives. We were involved in a circular process of biblical interpretation; our experience illuminated the Gospel narrative, and the Gospel, in turn, addressed our lives.

Luke's Portrait of Jesus

Jesus, the Saviour of the World

The Bible studies in this book are designed to explore the portrait Luke paints of Jesus. Of the several possible portraits in the Gospel itself, I have chosen to look at Luke's portrait of Jesus as the Saviour of the World. Of central importance will be discovering what kind of salvation Jesus brings. As the initial study says: Jesus is never the saviour we think he is! So who he brings his salvation to, what he says it is, what he demands of people who seek it, his relationship with the ruling class in Jerusalem, and the sustaining power behind his salvation are some of the features of Luke's portrait of Jesus which we will examine.

Ways to use this book

This book is intended primarily for use in group study but the material is presented in a way which makes it useful for individual study or as a resource for sermons, talks or workshops. The studies are structured in roughly the same way. They all include the biblical text under discussion (from the *New International Version*), background material or notes on the text, a discussion of the text, and some form of reflection. But the studies do differ in various respects. Some are thematic, studying a series of short texts from different parts of the Gospel. Sometimes there are texts from Acts; for the continuity between the Gospel and Acts makes Acts an important source for Luke's portrait of Jesus. Often a single passage is studied. But in all cases the intention is to discover Luke's portrait of Jesus as the Saviour.

The studies come from a specific South African context; they are unashamedly South African. In a similar way each person who reads this book will bring their specific context into play with the Gospel of Luke. Their reading of Luke will be unavoidably contextual. So, as you study Luke, allow *your* context to come to the fore. Don't let it influence your reading of Luke unconsciously. Debate with it, let it interact with the text. The success of this book depends on the extent to which you are able to take its insights and apply them to your own

24 Jesus, the Saviour of the World

lives and contexts; and, above all, on your willingness to respond to the call of Jesus the Saviour, to whom Luke bears witness.

Bible Studies
WHO BRINGS GOD'S SALVATION?

1. Jesus the Saviour Brings God's Salvation
Luke 2:11, 28-32

Background

Who is it who brings God's salvation? Who is God's agent of salvation? To most of us the answer to this question is so obvious that it makes asking the question a little absurd, for we all know who brings God's salvation — Jesus of course! Yet, for at least three reasons, it is an important question for us to ask. Firstly, because the Jews of Jesus' time asked it. Many of them expected salvation to come in the form of a Messiah, but fierce debates raged about who the Messiah really was and how and when he would come.

Further, it was a question that was being asked in the Hellenistic world. The profusion of religions in the Greco-Roman world is rivalled in history only by the profusion of religions in California today. The worship of the official gods of the Greek and Roman cities, the cult worship of the reigning Emperor, the mystery cults and the oriental cults made the religious scene a kaleidoscope of religious possibilities. So much so that we learn from one of Luke's other writings that there was an altar to the 'unknown god' (Acts 17:23) in Athens, a great religious and intellectual centre. Every possibility had to be covered. So for Luke, and for the community he was writing for, the question of true religion was of great importance. And the person who brought salvation — be it the Emperor, Bacchus, Artemis, Zeus or Jupiter, Isis, Cybele, the Jewish messiah or Jesus the Christ — would, of course, be the focus of much attention. So for the early Christian communities it was critical that this question be clearly settled. **Jesus**, not any other religious figure, was the one who brought God's salvation and Luke is concerned to make this clear to his community. Christianity was monotheistic. It did not share the open, pluralistic world view of the Roman empire with its multitude of religions.

And, finally, we need to ask the question because Jesus is never the kind of saviour we expect him to be. This was true for the Jews, it was true for the Romans and it remains true today. Sure, we know that Jesus is the saviour, but do we know what kind of saviour he is, what kind of salvation he brings? Our understanding of Jesus' salvation will at best always be partial. So we need constantly to seek to discover who he truly is. And the studies which follow will highlight some important aspects of Jesus' salvation. This study will do two things. Show why Jesus as saviour is an important theme in Luke, and ask the question, 'What kind of saviour are you looking for?'

> 2:11 **Today in the town of David a Saviour has been born to you; he is Christ the Lord.** 28 **Simeon took him [baby Jesus] in his arms and praised God, saying:** 29 **'Sovereign Lord, as you have promised, you now dismiss your servant in peace.** 30**For my eyes have seen your salvation,** 31**which you have prepared in the sight of all people,** 32**a light for revelation to the Gentiles and for glory to your people Israel.'**

Notes on the text

Is the concept of Jesus as saviour unique to Luke? Is it not the dominant theme throughout the New Testament?

Luke is the only one of the synoptic Gospels to actually use the word 'saviour'. Neither Matthew nor Mark use the word. Luke uses it twice in his Gospel and several times in Acts (Acts 5:31; 13:23), and John uses it only once. The first use of it is of God — 'my spirit rejoices in God my saviour' sings Mary (Luke 1:47). The second use of it refers to Jesus — 'today in the town of David a Saviour has been born to you; he is Christ the Lord' (Luke 2:11). Further, what makes this theme unique to Luke is that the word 'salvation' is exclusive to Luke. He uses it four times (Luke 1:69,71,77; 19:19), while John uses it once and Matthew and Mark not at all. Of the verb 'to save', all the Gospels have it but Luke more than any of them — eighteen times to Matthew's fourteen, Mark's eight, and John's six. While the number of times a word is used is not conclusive evidence of a major theme, it is a significant indication of what we might expect to find after further investigation.

Jesus the Saviour Brings God's Salvation

For Luke the events around Jesus' birth clearly demonstrate that this child who has come into the world is the one who will bring God's salvation. This becomes apparent if you look at the following passages: the Song of Zechariah (Luke 1:67-79, esp.69,71,77), the words of Simeon (Luke 2:28-32) and the preaching of John the Baptist (Luke 3:4-6).

For Luke, Jesus is quite clearly God's agent of salvation. His whole Gospel is written to acquaint his readers with this central fact. But Luke goes further than merely identifying Jesus as God's agent of salvation. That is merely the preliminary step — he goes on to demonstrate what kind of salvation this Jesus brings into the world.

Discussion: What kind of saviour are you looking for?

Salvation is a rich word, so much a part of our everyday religious language that it carries all kinds of meanings with it. Each time we see it we tend to read into it our own understanding of what it means, which is not necessarily the meaning the original writer intended. In a study like this our own definitions of salvation can be quite obstructive, for we may well be so attached to them and familiar with them that we are unable to give serious consideration to something which does not fit our own clearly held position. In order for us to have a coherent grasp of Luke's concept of salvation, we first need to be clear about what we understand salvation to be. You might think about this by actually writing down a definition of salvation. In a group these thoughts might be shared with others. You may wish to keep whatever is written down so that as this study progresses you can determine to what extent Luke's picture of Jesus' salvation matches yours. What kind of saviour are you looking for?

Reflection

At St Philip's we recognised that we, both as individuals and as a congregation, needed to be open to new aspects of God's salvation as we began this series of studies.

A Prayer

O God,
we can never fully comprehend
the fullness of the salvation you have brought to this world:
the depth of healing that it brings,
the defeat of evil and injustice it has achieved,

28 Jesus the Saviour Brings God's Salvation

the promise of new life that it offers.
Enable us as we study the Gospel of Luke
so to learn new facets of your salvation
and to experience your transforming power in our lives,
that we may be among those who bring the fullness of your salvation
   into this broken and tragic world.   Amen.

WHERE IS GOD'S SALVATION TO BE FOUND?

For many Jews in Jesus' time salvation was something that was expected in the future, something that had no immediate significance for their lives. Salvation lay in an expected event when God's messiah would come and restore the kingdom to Israel.

Many of the Gentile Christians who comprised Luke's wider audience may well have wondered about salvation as well. In a world which denigrated history and concrete human experience, the gods seldom came to earth. They seemed remote and distant, unconcerned with the affairs of the average person. When there was a 'human god' in the form of the Emperor he appeared even less accessible to the average individual in the enormous empire.

Today the historical Jesus seems far away. We may legitimately ask: 'So Jesus is God's agent of salvation. But he lived on earth about two thousand years ago. How does that help me today? Where do I find God's salvation?' And this question is most pertinently asked by those who endure sustained suffering.

In Luke's Gospel, Jesus, God's salvation, comes directly into political history and he intervenes in individual human lives. This is abundantly clear from the opening verses of the first three chapters of Luke, which will be the subject of the next two studies.

2. God's Salvation is Found in Political History
Luke 1:5-7; 2:1-6; 3:1-2

> 1:⁵In the time of Herod, king of Judea, there was a priest named Zechariah, who belonged to the division of Abijah; his wife Elizabeth was also a descendant of Aaron. ⁶Both of them were upright in the sight of God, observing all the Lord's commandments and regulations blamelessly. ⁷But they had no children, because Elizabeth was barren; and they were both well on in years.

30   God's Salvation is Found in Political History

2:¹In those days Caesar Augustus issued a decree that a census should be taken of the entire Roman world. ²(This was the first census that took place while Quirinius was governor of Syria.) ³And everyone went to his own town to register.

⁴So Joseph also went up from the town of Nazareth in Galilee to Judea, to Bethlehem the town of David, because he belonged to the house and line of David. ⁵He went there to register with Mary, who was pledged to be married to him and was expecting a child. ⁶While they were there the time came for the baby to be born, ⁷and she gave birth to her firstborn, a son. She wrapped him in strips of cloth and placed him in a manger, because there was no room for them in the inn.

3:¹In the fifteenth year of the reign of Tiberius Caesar - when Pontius Pilate was governor of Judea, Herod tetrarch of Galilee, his brother Philip tetrarch of Iturea and Trachonitis, and Lysanias tetrarch of Abilene — ²during the high-priesthood of Annas and Caiaphas, the word of God came to John son of Zechariah in the desert.

Notes on the texts

Each of these three readings have at least two things in common. I wonder whether you noticed what they are? Each passage contains both a description of a broad context, which is primarily political, as well as an account of the lives of individuals. Look at the passages again.

1:5-7 locates the event in 'the time of Herod king of Judea' (37-4 BCE) and is concerned with the lives of two individuals, Zechariah and Elizabeth (whose experiences we will study later inthe book). Caesar Augustus (27 BCE-14 CE) is the Emperor according to 2:1-6, while Quirinius was the governor of Syria. Moreover this was the time of the first census of Quirinius' governorship. The passage then focuses on the experience of two people: Mary and Joseph. The final passage, 3:1-2, gives a very developed picture of the political and religious powers of the day and then starts the story of John the Baptist.

This concern with locating the events the Gospels record in their broad historical context is unique to Luke. None of the other Gospels have this concern (see Mark 1:9, Matthew 2:1; 3:1 and John 1:1,19). We need to ask why Luke has this emphasis. As we noticed earlier, Luke was concerned with making the new Christian movement more acceptable to the Hellenistic world and the Roman authorities.

God's Salvation is Found in Political History 31

Locating events in their proper historical context was obviously important to him. It may have lent some credibility to his recounting of the origins of this movement of which he was a part.

Yet it also gives us insight into two things: that God's salvation occurs in the context of real life history and politics, as well as in the lives of people whose lives are just like ours.

Let us look at the different characters who appear in Luke 3:1-2 in a little more detail. Tiberius Caesar was the imperial overlord of the mighty Roman empire. He succeeded Augustus Caesar (Luke 2:1) in 14 CE, and wielded enormous power in Palestine. It was he who appointed Pontius Pilate to be governor of Judea, and Herod Antipas was responsible to him. Although Jesus never came close to having any direct dealings with Tiberius, it was Tiberius' image on the coin which Jesus used to answer the question of taxes (Luke 20:23-25).

Pontius Pilate was procurator of Judea for ten years. The posting to Jerusalem was a difficult one in the Roman colonial office, for Judea was known for its simmering unrest, its uneasy political tensions, and its remarkably delicate religious sensibilities. It was a tough job which demanded someone who could maintain a strong hold over things, without inflaming the delicate situation. The Judeans resisted Rome's oppression to such an extent that in 70 CE the Roman authorities decided to destroy Jerusalem. Pilate, as the governor of Judea, was the central point of Roman control in Judea. He represented the Roman colonial power, the Roman soldiers and the Roman tax collectors. Great economic and political power rested in his hands.

Herod Antipas, and the Herodian family as a whole, were collaborators with the Roman imperial power. Because they were native Palestinians they were regarded by many as sell-outs to the regime to which they owed their exalted status. Antipas' unpopularity is demonstrated by the major political riots and upheavals that swept Galilee in 4 CE when he went to Rome to be appointed King of Galilee by Caesar Augustus.

Jewish religious and political control in Judea was centred in the Sanhedrin under the leadership of the high priests, who Luke records as being Annas and Caiaphas. Annas was a very influential high priest, appointed in 6 CE and deposed by the Romans in 15 CE. Caiaphas, Annas' son-in-law, was high priest from 18 to 36 CE,

32 God's Salvation is Found in Political History

which covered the period of Jesus' trial. While the Romans deposed high priests and appointed new ones, the Jews thought of the high priesthood as a life office — which may explain why Luke speaks of both Annas and Caiaphas as high priest. Just as Pilate and Herod Antipas represented a very specific form of economic and political power in Palestine, so too did Annas and Caiaphas. Their power and authority derived from their control of the temple and of the Sanhedrin, the ruling body in all aspects of Jewish life.

Luke intentionally locates the birth stories of Jesus and the start of Jesus' ministry in a very specific political context for he shows how, later on, Jesus and his disciples interacted dramatically with these political realities. [Studies 11 and 12 are of particular importance for this theme.]

Discussion

It is important for us to analyse *our* political and religious context, for this is the context in which God's salvation comes to us today.

One of the exercises we did at St Philip's was to spell out our context using the categories of Luke 3:1-2. We came up with the following chart.

Luke 3:1 — 24:53	St Philip's 1986-1987
Tiberius Caesar (14-37 CE) 15th year = 29 CE	38th year of Nationalist Government (1948-1986)
Galilee: Herod Antipas (4 BCE-39 CE) Judea: Pontius Pilate (26-36 CE)	President: P.W. Botha Minister of Police: Louis le Grange
High Priests: Caiaphas and Annas	Anglican Archbishops: Philip Russel and Desmond Tutu

The primary political reference for St Philip's was undoubtably the Nationalist government with its apartheid policies. Since 1985 the struggle for a just society and the ending of Nationalist party rule has reached such proportions that the President declared a State of Emergency. This gave enormous powers to the police and military

God's Salvation is Found in Political History 33

forces to maintain political control of the country. Minister of Police Louis le Grange emerged as one of the key figures in the massive and violent clampdown on any real opposition to the apartheid regime. Tens of thousands of people were detained without trial, hundreds of civilians were killed and thousands wounded by the police and the military forces. The oppression of the majority of people in South Africa was re-enforced, while the comfort of the minority further protected.

The congregation of St Philip's was deeply affected by this political turmoil. Many of the congregation are school teachers who witnessed the severe brutality of the police as they repeatedly stormed student gatherings and meetings. A number of these teachers were themselves the victims of police violence. One of the young members of the congregation is at present in jail for a year on charges of public violence, a charge which has been widely criticised. Cape Town's squatter camp, Crossroads, erupted into state-manipulated violence in the winter of 1986 with thousands of poverty stricken people losing all their meagre possessions. St Philip's church hall became a refugee centre for some of these people, who were housed there for several months. Their presence in our church hall made the experience of the radically poor and oppressed part of the context for our worship and life as a congregation.

This was the context in which we, as a worshipping community, had to ask what God's salvation was. Clearly it had to be related to the political situation that was causing so much pain and anguish for thousands in our country.

In 1986 Desmond Tutu was elected Archbishop of Cape Town. His election was greeted with great joy at St Philip's for he represented the struggle of the Church against the precise causes of the political conflict. His appointment was so different to that of Annas and Caiaphas in Jesus' time, for they were appointees of the Roman authorities. Luke makes it quite clear that they were the key figures in Jesus' arrest and death (Luke 19:47). In Desmond Tutu, the Church voted against political oppression and voted for liberation, for God's true salvation. On this point the Church and the State were at conflict.

Reflection
As a reflection you might map out your political and religious

34 God's Salvation is Found in Political History

situation in the way in which we did in the chart on p.00. What are the critical issues at stake in your country and how is your church responding to them? Do you think that God's salvation has anything concrete to do with political situations? If so, in what way does this take place? Does it come in judgement or in restoration?

Luke definitely has Jesus on the broad sweep of political developments. As we progress through this book we will see how this works out in Jesus' life and in practice. That God is involved in the political affairs of the world is a basic assumption in the Old Testament. This is especially true of the prophets and of many of the Psalms. At St Philip's we prayerfully read from Isaiah 14 to remind ourselves of how God acts in political history. It was our earnest prayer that God would act like that in South Africa.

Isaiah 14:4-7,22-27
How the oppressor has come to an end!
How his fury has ended!
The Lord has broken the rod of the wicked,
   the sceptre of the rulers,
which in anger struck down peoples
   with unceasing blows,
and in fury subdued the nations
   with relentless aggression.
All the lands are at rest and at peace;
   they break into singing.

'I will rise up against them,'
   declares the Lord Almighty.
'I will cut off from Babylon her name and survivors,
   her offspring and her descendants,'
declares the Lord.

'I will turn her into a place for owls
   and into swampland;
I will sweep her with the broom of destruction,'
   declares the Lord the Almighty.

The Lord Almighty has sworn,

'Surely, as I have planned it, so will it be,

and as I have purposed, so it will stand.
I will crush the Assyrian in my land;
   on my mountain I will trample him down.
His yoke will be taken from my people,
   and his burden removed from their shoulders.'

This is the plan determined for the whole world;
   this is the hand stretched out over all nations.
For the Lord Almighty has purposed, and who can thwart him?
   His hand is stretched out, and who can turn it back?

3. God's Salvation is Found in Human Experience

Luke 1:5-7; 2:1-6; 3:1-2

In this study we return to the three passages we looked at in the previous study, for, as we noticed, they addressed not only the broad political context in which God's salvation appeared, but also referred to the experience of individual people. Let us re-read them and notice how each refers to a particular experience in the lives of certain individuals. These individual lives are set by Luke in the context of political history, for all lives are lived in the midst of history. This understanding is crucial to Luke's portrait of Jesus.

Readings
For the readings refer back to the previous study (pp. 29-30).

Notes on the text
1:5-7. Having set the political context for the events which are to follow, Luke, without further ado, begins his Gospel by telling the story of a childless couple, Zechariah and Elizabeth. Zechariah was a priest, low down in the priestly hierarchy. He was a member of one of the twenty-four divisions of priests that served in the temple in Jerusalem for one week every six months. The couple lived in one of the towns outside Jerusalem (see Luke 1:39,40) with Zechariah going into the city for his twice-yearly period of service. Elizabeth, like Zechariah, belonged to a priestly family. Well on in years, this couple must have long given up hope for a child of their own. The personal pain they felt was compounded by the social stigma of barrenness which Elizabeth had to endure. (We look at her story in detail in study 7.) Luke's account does not stop here of course; he goes on to tell the story of the conception and birth of John the Baptist. But I wish to highlight the way Luke's Gospel begins with a poignant story of an elderly couple who had no children.

Contrast this with the other Gospels. Matthew opens with a genealogy and a rather brusque account of Jesus' birth (Matthew 1:1-24). Mark has no birth stories but plunges right into a hectic series of events: the preaching of John the Baptist, Jesus' baptism and temptation and the calling of the first disciples. And, of course, John opens

God's Salvation is Found in Human Experience

with that sublime statement of the pre-existence of the Word of God. Luke is quite different. An immensely personal touch characterises the long opening chapters of this Gospel.

In the second passage (Luke 2:1-6) our attention is drawn to another couple, this time a young couple who have to journey from Galilee in the North to a village in Judea in the South because of a census that is taking place. Joseph, as a descendant of King David, has to return to Bethlehem to be registered there. He takes with him his fiancé, Mary. She is in the last stages of her pregnancy when they arrive in what is for her a strange town. There she gives birth to her first child in a stable, far from all that is familiar, far from the security of home and family. Here the issue is not barrenness but an untimely birth. (Mary's story will be looked at in detail in study 8.) Luke has, in the previous chapter, made it clear what kind of a pregnancy this is, but he never allows the element of divine intervention to obscure the reality of the human experience into which God's salvation comes.

The third passage (Luke 3:1)2) focuses on a young man who hears God's word in the desert. John, the son of the once barren Elizabeth and Zechariah, responds to God's word by embarking on a mission of preaching in the area around the Jordan river. Luke, like the other evangelists, casts John in the mould of an Old Testament prophet; one who calls people to repentance, and who not surprisingly soon lands up in prison because of his criticism of the king — in this case Herod Antipas, son of Herod the Great. But, characteristically, Luke gives John more personality than the other Gospels. As we have seen, he gives an intimate view of the events surrounding John's birth and is the only one who tells of John's call. He also gives John's preaching more content than the other Gospel writers (Luke 3:3-20. See also Luke 7:18-35). John is an individual, not merely a figure like an Old Testament prophet. And it is to this individual that God's Word comes.

Discussion

At the beginning of the first three chapters of Luke's Gospel we find him highlighting the experience of individual people. God's salvation comes to individuals.

Look through the Gospel of Luke and notice how consistently Jesus deals with individuals, meeting them at their point of need. As you turn the pages you will see him heal, liberate and encourage many people. Jesus is the comforter to those whose lives are destitute of hope. He brings peace and wholeness to the troubled of this world. But there are also those who turn away from Jesus, sad because they cannot meet his radical challenge to their lives, for his call to discipleship is costly indeed.

In Luke's Gospel we see God's salvation come to and through Elizabeth and Mary. We meet Jesus with people possessed by demons, Peter's sick mother-in-law, fishermen at their nets, lepers, a tax collector, the Pharisees, a Roman army general, a widow and her son, Zacchaeus and a rich ruler. Jesus meets all these people as individuals and confronts them with the salvation he brings. But we always see him in personal interaction with the people he meets. And the people he meets are not unlike us. It is this fact which makes us able to read the Gospels and to encounter Jesus.

Reflection

Jesus comes to us just as personally as he came to the people Luke wrote about. Spend some time asking yourself at what point in your life is Jesus meeting you at the moment. Does he come as one who brings a challenge, or is it as one who brings comfort? It would be useful too to reflect on how he has met you in the past. The Psalms are full of this type of reflection.

Psalm 116:1-7
I love the Lord, for he heard my voice;
    he heard my cry for mercy.
Because he turned his ear to me,
    I will call on him as long as I live.

The cords of death entangled me,
    the anguish of the grave came upon me;
I was overcome by trouble and sorrow.
Then I called on the name of the Lord:
    'O Lord, save me!'

The Lord is gracious and righteous;
    our God is full of compassion.
The Lord protects the simple-hearted;
    when I was in great need, he saved me.

Be at rest once more, O my soul,
   for the Lord has been good to you.

4. Jesus' Manifesto of Salvation
Luke 4:14-30

4:¹⁴Jesus returned to Galilee in the power of the Spirit, and news about him spread through the whole countryside. ¹⁵He taught in their synagogues, and everybody praised him. ¹⁶He went to Nazareth, where he had been brought up, and on the Sabbath day he went into the synagogue, as was his custom. And he stood up to read. ¹⁷The scroll of the prophet Isaiah was handed to him. Unrolling it, he found the place where it is written:
¹⁸'The Spirit of the Lord is on me,
because he has anointed me
to preach good news to the poor.
He has sent me to proclaim
   freedom for the prisoners
and recovery of sight for the blind,
to release the oppressed,
¹⁹to proclaim the year of the Lord's favour.'
²⁰Then he rolled up the scroll, gave it back to the attendant and sat down. The eyes of everyone in the synagogue were fastened on him, ²¹and he began by saying to them, 'Today this scripture is fulfilled in your hearing.'

Notes on the passage

This passage is one of the more distinctive passages in the Gospel of Luke for two reasons. It is not found in any of the other Gospels, and it contains some of the themes special to Luke's portrait of Jesus. Luke chooses to record this incident as the first detailed event after Jesus' temptation in the desert. He uses it as the focal point for the start of Jesus' public activity; an incident in which Jesus explains what he understands his function on earth to be. Matthew and Mark, in contrast, begin Jesus' public ministry with the calling of the disciples, which Luke narrates after this event in the synagogue.

Luke recounts the event as a statement of calling or purpose. Jesus reads a passage from Isaiah 61, a passage filled with messianic significance, and states that the passage has been fulfilled by him. He is the one whom the Spirit of the Lord has anointed, who is sent to preach good news, to proclaim freedom for the prisoners. This is the ministry to which he has been called. For Luke the rest of Jesus' life is an exposition of this passage, putting into practice what he said he was sent to do. This is something which we need constantly to bear in mind as we follow the development of the portrait of Jesus in the Gospel.

Before we focus on the central part of the text, 4:18-19, a few general comments will be useful. Firstly, notice Luke's stress on the role of the Holy Spirit in Jesus' life. Luke 3 ends with Jesus being baptised and the Holy Spirit descending on him like a dove (Luke 3:22). Luke 4 begins with Jesus, full of the Holy Spirit, returning from the baptism in the river Jordan. He is then led by the Spirit into the desert where he is to face the temptations. After the temptations Jesus returns from the desert to Galilee, his home country, 'in the power of the Spirit' (4:14). And in the passage from Isaiah 61 which Jesus reads in the synagogue, it is the 'Spirit of the Lord' who anoints and sends God's chosen agent of liberation (4:18). This stress on Jesus' dependence on the Spirit is characteristic of Luke and will be the subject of independent discussion in the next study. Luke's second volume, Acts, shares this concern with the Spirit who is seen to be the one who guides and empowers the early Church in its most formative stages. What is important for us in this study is to realise that Luke clearly links the Holy Spirit with Jesus' statement of purpose. The salvation which Jesus brings is salvation which is empowered by the Holy Spirit.

Secondly, the cultural significance of what Jesus did in the synagogue requires some explanation. Jesus as an adult Jewish male had the right, by invitation of the president of the synagogue, to read the scriptures on the Sabbath day. In Jesus' time the readings from the Law (the first five books of the Hebrew Bible) were prescribed according to a lectionary. This was not the case for the Prophets. As was his custom, Jesus went to the synagogue on the Sabbath and was chosen to read from the Prophets. As 4:15 indicates, he had been teaching in synagogues in Galilee and so we may assume that he was expected to do the same in Nazareth, especially since we are told that the congregation waited in an attitude of expectation following his reading: (4:20). '. . . news had spread about him through the whole-countryside . . .' (4:14). The people of Nazareth must have been eager to hear what their much talked-about fellow Nazareen would say in his home village. After the reading he began his sermon with the astonishing, and to his hearers, quite blasphemous words, 'Today this scripture is fulfilled in your hearing' (4:21). Luke portrays Jesus as self-consciously identifying himself as the one who fulfils this prophecy; it was he whom God had chosen to announce the year of the Lord's favour, the coming of God's salvation to the world and to God's people.

Discussion

What do we learn about Luke's portrait of Jesus? Firstly, we learn that Luke understood that Jesus identified himself as the one who fulfilled Jewish messianic expectations. Secondly, the role of this messiah, or the servant of God, is given very particular definition. He is the one who has been chosen to:
preach good news to the poor
proclaim freedom for the prisoners
and recovery of sight to the blind,
release the oppressed,
proclaim the year of the Lord's favour.

What was Jesus really saying here? When asked this question, the night we studied this text, the people at St Philip's understood the words in spiritual terms only. The poor were the poor in spirit; the captives were captives to the devil and to this world; the blind were those who did not believe; the oppressed were the spiritually oppressed, or religiously persecuted. Not many knew what 'the acceptable year of the Lord' meant. I think this is a fair representation of the interpretation of this passage that one might find in the average church in South Africa.

The debate about the meaning of this passage is fairly complex and involves such issues as the meaning of Isaiah 61 and the meaning of individual words. Luke, however, makes the task easy for us. Let's look at Luke 7:18-23, for in this passage Luke gives some clear indications as to what he understood these words to mean. In this passage John the Baptist, by now in prison, sends some of his followers to ask Jesus if he was the one whom the Jews expected, namely, the Messiah. We pick the text up at verse 21.

> 7:²¹At that very time Jesus cured many who had diseases, sicknesses and evil spirits, and gave sight to many who were blind.

> [22]So he replied to the messengers, 'Go back and report to John what you have seen and heard: The blind receive sight, the lame walk, those who have leprosy are cured, the deaf hear, the dead are raised, and the good news is preached to the poor. [23]Blessed is the person who does not fall away on account of me.'

In his reply Jesus demonstrates to John the Baptist's messengers that his ministry cannot be understood in purely spiritual terms. He has come to heal the physical ailments of suffering people. And this is the sign that he is the one who has been expected. This is where the messiah is to be found: among the blind, the lame, the lepers, the deaf and the poor. God's salvation comes through Jesus to the suffering of the world.

Recent studies of the diseases which Jesus encountered, including demon possession, indicate that they are diseases which are common to most politically and economically oppressed groups. These diseases are physiological expressions of the social and psychological stress which often accompany the hardship of poverty and the stress of oppression. Jesus, in his reply to John the Baptist, identified his mission on earth with people who suffered such afflictions. It is to such people that Luke's Jesus came; he would give up his life for them in Jerusalem as he attacked the oppressive ruling class for the way in which they treated the poor.

In contrast to this identification with the poor and the suffering, the Lukan Jesus meets people of wealth or privilege only at their initiative. His initiative is to the poor. And his relationship with the powerful classes of Palestine is characterised by conflict. (This will become clear in studies 9 and 12.)

Reflection

For us at St Philip's it was abundantly clear just who the poor, the prisoners, the blind and the oppressed were in our society. The poor were living in the hall of our church; people without homes, without jobs, without security and with meagre possessions. The oppressed were the twenty-five million black people in the country who were at the mercy of the racist and exploitative structures of the powerful. And many of us at St Philip's knew what this oppression meant. Prisoners filled the prisons of our land; many thousands of them never having faced trial. And our hearts grew heavy as we thought of those we knew who were in prison. Yet we were conscious of how

Patrick Holo

44   Jesus' Manifesto of Salvation

little we believed that Jesus identified himself with these people and with those of us who were poor, oppressed or imprisoned.

A Liturgy of Confession and Petition

Leader   God, in this country:

All   We have seen families displaced, with no home, no money and no place to go.
We have seen persons broken, humiliated and imprisoned simply because they are black.
We have seen children shot dead, detained and tortured because they refused to be broken.
We have seen children die of malnutrition in a rich and fertile country.
We have seen so much suffering, so much pain, so much despair, so much fear and so much anger.
And there are of us those who have borne some of these ills ourselves.

Leader   Righteous Judge, forgive us we pray:

All   For denying in our words and in our actions that it is to these anguished of the earth that you come.
For refusing to live as you lived; a life given in service of others.
For being complacent when we are comfortable; closing our eyes to the pain of others.
For refusing to believe that you are with us when we ourselves suffer.

Leader   Grant us Creator God:

All   Strength to resist all that is evil.
Hope that endures what ever we may face.
Love which drives us to live for others.

Leader   Almighty God who loves justice and hates evil:

All   Bring down unjust rulers from their thrones.
Scatter the proud and lift up the humble.
Send the rich away empty and fill the hungry with good things.
Defend the powerless and frustrate the oppressor.

May your kingdom come on earth as it is in heaven.
Amen.

JESUS' SALVATION COMES IN POWER AND WEAKNESS

Luke portrays Jesus as one who is both super human and simply human. He is portrayed as an immensely authoritative figure, filled with the power which God has given him through the Holy Spirit. He wrestles with and defeats the devil in the desert; he teaches with authority; challenges the rulers of Palestine; casts out demons and is always in control. But he is intensely human as well. He weeps over Jerusalem, his compassion for the suffering knows no bounds, and in the garden of Gethsemane his anguish makes him sweat drops like blood.

5. The Holy Spirit Empowers Jesus' Salvation
Luke 1:34,35; 2:25-28; 3:21-23; 4:1,2,14,18,31-37; 12:11,12

No adequate description of Luke's portrait of Jesus is possible without a discussion of the role of the Spirit in the Gospel, for more than in any other Gospel Luke has made the Holy Spirit an important facet of his portrait of Jesus. Simple statistics indicate Luke's concentration on the Spirit; the Spirit is mentioned seventeen times in Luke, as opposed to twelve in Matthew, four in Mark and fifteen in John; the Spirit also appears fifty-seven times in Luke's second volume, Acts. In this study we will see that Luke portrays Jesus as one who is empowered by the Holy Spirit for his mission on earth.

> 1:[34]'How will this be,' Mary asked the angel, 'since I am a virgin?' [35]The angel answered, 'The Holy Spirit will come upon you, and the power of the Most High will overshadow you. So the holy one to be born will be called the Son of God.'
>
> 2:[25]Now there was a man in Jerusalem called Simeon, who was righteous and devout. He was waiting for the consolation of Israel, and the Holy Spirit was upon him. [26]It had been revealed to him by the Holy Spirit that he would not die before he had seen the Lord's Christ. [27]Moved by the Spirit, he went into the temple courts.

When the parents brought the child Jesus to do for him what the custom of the Law required, ²⁸Simeon took him in his arms and praised God.

3:²¹When all the people were being baptised, Jesus was baptised too. And as he was praying, heaven was opened ²²and the Holy Spirit descended on him in bodily form like a dove. And a voice came from heaven; 'You are my Son, whom I love; with you I am well pleased.' ²³Now Jesus himself was about thirty years old when he began his ministry.

4:¹Jesus, full of the Holy Spirit, returned from the Jordan and was led by the Spirit in the desert, ²where for forty days he was tempted by the devil . . . ¹⁴Jesus returned to Galilee in the power of the Spirit, and news about him spread through the whole countryside . . . ¹⁸'The Spirit of the Lord is on me, because he has anointed me to preach . . . He has sent me to proclaim . . . ³¹Then he went down to Capernaum, a town in Galilee, and on the Sabbath began to teach the people. ³²They were amazed at his teaching because his message had authority. ³³In the synagogue there was a man possessed by a demon, an evil spirit. He cried out at the top of his voice, ³⁴'Ha! What do you want with us, Jesus of Nazareth? Have you come to destroy us? I know who you are — the Holy One of God!' ³⁵'Be quiet!' Jesus said sternly. 'Come out of him!' Then the demon threw the man down before them all and came out without injuring him. ³⁶All the people were amazed and said to each other, 'What is this teaching? With what authority and power he gives orders to evil spirits and they come out!' ³⁷And the news about him spread throughout the surrounding area.

12:¹¹'When you are brought before synagogues, rulers and authorities, do not worry about how you will defend yourselves or what you will say, ¹²for the Holy Spirit will teach you at that time what you should say.'

Notes on the texts

1:34,35   From the beginning of his Gospel Luke links the Holy Spirit to power. The power of the Most High comes with the Holy Spirit and Mary conceives. The Holy Spirit is with Jesus from the moment of conception. For the rest of his life Jesus will have the Spirit to empower him for his calling on earth.

2:25-28   In this passage there are three references to the Holy Spirit. Luke stresses that it is the Holy Spirit, speaking through

The Holy Spirit Empowers Jesus' Salvation

Simeon, who confirms that the birth of Jesus is the birth of the messiah. The word, Christ, 'anointed one', is the Greek form of the Hebrew word for messiah. Luke wants to make it abundantly clear to his readers just who Jesus is. And it is the Spirit who inspires these words of confirmation. Jesus is not only conceived by the Holy Spirit, but his birth is confirmed by the Holy Spirit.

3:21-23   In Luke, the baptism of Jesus starts a series of events which mark the beginning of Jesus' ministry. Jesus can only begin this ministry once he has been baptised, and more importantly for Luke, once he has received God's blessing and the Holy Spirit has come upon him.

4:1,2   Jesus was baptised in the river Jordan. From there the Spirit led him into the desert where he not only fasted for forty days but was involved in an intense struggle with the devil. It is because he went into this struggle filled with the Holy Spirit that he is able to defeat the devil.

4:14   Immediately after the episode in the desert, Jesus returns to Galilee in the power of the Spirit. What is of note here for Luke is, once again, the link between power and the Holy Spirit. The power that Jesus demonstrates in his life comes from the Holy Spirit; the Holy Spirit not only anoints Jesus to be the saviour, but empowers Jesus to be the saviour. Full of the power of the Holy Spirit he begins his ministry in Galilee.

4:18   For comment on this verse see the previous study.

4:31-37   Very soon after he returns from the struggle in the desert, Jesus encounters the devil once again; this time in a man possessed by an evil spirit. Because Jesus is filled with the Spirit he teaches with authority; and with authority and power casts out demons. This is the first of four exorcism stories in Luke (the others are 8:26-39; 9:37-43; and 11:14-26). They are used by Luke to demonstrate the power which Jesus has. The link between the Holy Spirit and the casting out of demons is made clear in Acts 10:37,38:

> 'You know what has happened throughout Judea, beginning in Galilee after the baptism that John preached — how God anointed Jesus of Nazareth with the Holy Spirit and power, and how he went around doing good and healing all who were under the power of the devil, because God was with him.'

48 The Holy Spirit Empowers Jesus' Salvation

The power of the devil is pitted against the power of Jesus which comes from the Holy Spirit.

12:11,12   In Luke's Gospel, Jesus assumes that his disciples are going to suffer the same fate as him; appearing before governors and authorities on trial. And this certainly is the case as Luke later demonstrates in Acts; the apostles are repeatedly on trial, imprisoned and even, like Stephen, put to death. Luke's readers would easily have identified with this as they too often faced persecution. In this situation Jesus speaks words of comfort; the Holy Spirit will be with his disciples when they are on trial and will give them the words to speak.

Discussion

Luke paints Jesus as one who was driven and empowered by the Holy Spirit. He is more than human; his authority and power astound people for they are not used to this kind of person. But the remarkable thing about this driving Spirit is that Jesus is constantly driven into conflict. He moves straight from the baptism into conflict with the devil in the desert. Straight from the desert to reading in the synagogue — which sparks off conflict with his fellow Nazareens, and immediately on to conflict with an evil spirit. The salvation which the Holy Spirit inspires is a salvation which conflicts with evil. This Holy Spirit gives a power that disturbs; not even the demons can rest easy, for the Holy Spirit comes to free people from the shackles of their distorted psyches.

So it is no surprise that when Jesus teaches his disciples about the Holy Spirit he assumes that they too will be in conflict. 'When [not "if"] you are brought before synagogues, rulers and authorities . . .' says Jesus. Then the Holy Spirit will give you the words to speak. In his second volume Luke shows how this became the experience of the early Christians. 'The next day the rulers, elders and teachers of the law met in Jerusalem. . . . They had Peter and John brought before them and began to question them. . . . Then Peter, filled with the Holy Spirit, said to them: Rulers and elders of the people!' (Acts 4:5,7,8. See also Acts 6:8,12; 7:54,55; 24:1-26:32.) The Holy Spirit will be there when you appear before the authorities.

Reflection

Many of us at St Philip's recognised that we for too long confined the

Holy Spirit to a particular realm of our experience. To us, the Spirit was the one who gave spiritual gifts to the Church; gifts of prophecy, teaching, interpretations, tongues, healing. The Spirit's presence was known by the fruits the Christian displayed; love, joy, peace, patience, kindness, goodness, faithfulness, gentleness and self-control. But we had never thought of the Spirit indirectly, in terms of appearing before magistrates or rulers; in terms of the Wynberg or Athlone magistrates court. We knew these places well but somehow had failed to understand that this was one place where Jesus had promised the Holy Spirit would be.

So we prayed that God would fill us with the power of the Holy Spirit; knowing that this would lead us into a life of greater conflict with evil. And secure in the knowledge that when this conflict took us to the courts of this country, we would be empowered by the Holy Spirit.

We believed that the Holy Spirit was available to those who asked, for had Jesus not said:
> Which of you parents, if your child asks for a fish, will give your child a snake instead? Or if your child asks for an egg, will give a scorpion? If you then, though you are evil, know how to give good gifts to your children, how much more will God, your parent in heaven, give the Holy Spirit to those who ask! (Luke 11:11-13.)

Now to God who is able to do immeasurably more than we can ask or think, according to the Spirit's power which is at work within us, to God be glory in the Church and in Christ Jesus throughout all generations for ever and ever! Amen.

6. Prayer: the Human Cry for Deliverance
Luke 22:39-44; 18:1-8

Prayer is a strange, wonderful and illusive thing. It lies at the heart of the Christian faith yet for many it remains an enigma; strangely, both rewarding and futile. It has taken people to the heights of religious experience; calmed and strengthened those in extreme fear and been a constant sustaining experience in the lives of untold multitudes. But for others it has been a burden under which they have laboured; an expectation dimmed through constant disappointment; a futility long since discarded.

With these varied experiences of prayer in mind, we turned to look at prayer in Luke's Gospel as the cry for salvation. (It might be an idea to spend sometime reflecting or talking about your own experiences of prayer before proceeding to the text.)

> 22:³⁹Jesus went out as usual to the Mount of Olives, and his disciples followed him. ⁴⁰On reaching the place, he said to them, 'Pray that you will not fall into temptation.' ⁴¹He withdrew about a stone's throw beyond them, knelt down and prayed, ⁴²'Father, if you are willing, take this cup from me; yet not my will, but yours be done.' ⁴³An angel from heaven appeared to him and strengthened him. ⁴⁴And being in anguish, he prayed more earnestly, and his sweat was like drops of blood falling to the ground.
>
> 18:¹Then Jesus told his disciples a parable to show them that they should always pray and not give up. ²He said: 'In a certain town there was a judge who neither feared God nor cared about men. ³And there was a widow in that town who kept coming to him with the plea, "Grant me justice against my adversary." ⁴For some time he refused. But finally he said to himself, "Even though I don't fear God or care about men, ⁵yet because this widow keeps on bothering me, I will see that she gets justice, so that she won't eventually wear me out with her coming!"' ⁶And the Lord said, 'Listen to what the unjust judge says. ⁷And will not God bring about justice for his chosen ones, who cry out to him day and night? Will he keep putting them off? ⁸I tell you, he will see that they get justice and quickly. However, when the Son of Man comes, will he find faith on the earth?'

Notes on the texts

The texts for this study reflect two aspects of prayer; Jesus at prayer and his teaching on prayer.

Jesus at prayer: 22:39-44

Luke often depicts Jesus in prayer. He explicitly links many of the major episodes in Jesus' life to prayer, a feature unique to his portrait. Accordingly, at Jesus' baptism (3:21), before choosing the twelve apostles (6:12), before the first announcement of his coming death

(9:18), at his transfiguration (9:28), before he teaches the 'Our Father' (11:2), during his agony before the crucifixion (22:41) and on the cross itself (23:46), Jesus is at prayer.

22:39 Luke simply states that Jesus went to the Mount of Olives. Matthew (26:36) and Mark (14:32) are more specific; they have Jesus going to a place called Gethsemane on the Mount of Olives.

22:42 'Father take this cup from me.' 'Cup' carries the rich Old Testament sense of the cup of destiny; the cup of God's wrath, his judgement upon the evil nations of the world (Isaiah 51:17,22; Jeremiah 25:15-29). Jesus has reached the point of his destiny: his conflict with the ruling class of Jerusalem is about to result in his crucifixion. Now he is to drink this most painful cup.

22:43,44 These verses are omitted in some versions of the Bible (see R.S.V.) because many of the important manuscripts from which we construct the text of Luke do not have them. As we are using the N.I.V., we will assume they are part of Luke.

22:44 Jesus does not sweat blood, as is sometimes believed; but rather his sweat was *like* blood; thick drops of it falling to the ground.

Jesus' teaching on prayer: 18:1-8
According to the Gospel of Luke a central characteristic of Christian discipleship is prayer; and Jesus not only provides an example of this in his own life but he often teaches about prayer. Luke is the only Gospel writer who records the disciples asking to be taught how to pray (11:1), to which Jesus responds by teaching the 'Our Father' (11:2-4). More of Jesus' teaching on prayer is found in 11:5-13, 10:2, and 18:9-14.

18:3 Widows play a special role in Luke's writings. As in the Old Testament (Exodus 22:22-24; Ruth 1:20-21; Isaiah 54:4: Psalm 68:5) widows are pictured as people to whom justice is denied. Widows, in particular, were vulnerable to exploitation because in Palestinian society they were helpless as women alone in a male dominated society. Persistence was their only weapon. Widows feature in Luke 2:37; 4:25-26; 7:12; 20:47; 21:2-3 and in Acts 6:1; 9:39,41.

Discussion
Two dimensions of prayer dominate these two texts; prayer as an

expression of profound anguish and prayer as the persistent cry of the oppressed.

Nowhere in the Gospel account is Jesus more human than in Gethsemane on the Mount of Olives. In his anguished prayer Jesus expresses his deepest pain and the loathing he feels about what is about to take place, the physical suffering and the psychological stress. Jesus well knows the horror of crucifixion. Compounding this must be some inner distress and doubt about the meaning of it all. Was this really the way to accomplish the salvation he was bringing to earth? And so he prays; 'Father, if you are willing take this cup from me; yet not my will, but yours be done.' Jesus' salvation was to cost him an agonising death on the cross. Small wonder that he could call the rich ruler to give up all his wealth. The expectation of what is about to happen brings a physical revulsion; he sweats drops of sweat like blood.

In this prayer Jesus' humanity emerges at its fullest. He is human to the very core; the death facing him nauseates him. His prayer is a cry for deliverance. He reveals his most intimate personal response to God's plan for his life. The cup seems too bitter for him to swallow.

The second example of prayer is also a cry for deliverance. Here it is the cry of an oppressed woman, a widow; it is the cry of God's oppressed children for justice. Jesus tells his disciples to be persistent like the widow. Neither she nor the judge will know peace until she finds justice. This persistence, Jesus says, will be speedily rewarded; God will see that they get justice.

Reflection
In these texts prayer is expressed in two ways; an individual's expression of deep personal anguish and the consistent and sustained petition of the oppressed. In one of the more remarkable experiences of my life I found something of these two features combined. Use the story to reflect on what prayer is; what it expresses and what it means when persistence is not rewarded.

It was in the winter of 1981. Typically, it was in the cold, driving rain of winter that the government authorities began destroying the rudimentary shacks of the squatters' camp near Cape Town's renowned Crossroads.

Their purpose: to force these unwelcome black people back to the impoverished 'homelands' they had fled, coming to the city in desperation hoping to eke out a living on the city's periphery.

This year the squatters refused to move. In place of the rudimentary corrugated iron structures bulldozed down by the Bantu Administration Board (BAB) officials, they erected structures more flimsy yet; builder's plastic drawn over boughs of Port Jackson willow stuck into the sandy ground. Under these shelters the squatter community spent the long, cold, wet nights. In the mornings they dismantled their 'homes' in the seeping drizzle, and moved what belongings they had to a safer place so that their plastic, their boughs of Port Jackson, their blankets and food would not be confiscated by the government. And so the litany went on. In their solidarity, in their refusal to move, in their defiance of injustice, the community would not be cowed.

In a humble and somewhat belated response to this act of defiance, churches began to send in food, blankets and clothing; material support for the pride of those who refused to be trampled down. Two of us slept with the community to monitor the activity of the government officials. One night, a deputy editor of a large Johannesburg newspaper was smuggled in. Listening to the people praying and singing he remarked, cynically; 'This is the worst about religion. It keeps oppressed people passive.'

Very early in the morning the rain came down with a vengeance. Some of us woke wet and cold, got up and sought refuge in the cook tent near the warm fire where, huddled up, we listened to the women preparing breakfast, singing a plaintive song of appeal to God. The refrain was the words of Jesus on the cross; 'Eloi, Eloi, lama sabachthani? My God, my God, why have you forsaken me?' Their pain filled words dropped like blood into the mud. The mud, the rain, the hissing, spurting fire was their Gethsemane.

Suddenly, at 4:30 in the morning, the unexpected noise of the government trucks shattered the uneasy peace of the camp. Grinding their way through the mud they surrounded the camp, their headlights burning down on the confusion. Backed by the baying of dogs and rifled police, the BAB officials waded in and ripped the shelters down. The cook tent went down and that morning's porridge mingled with the mud.

An hour later on the lonely, desolated hillock stood a group of the squatters. They were praying and singing; begging God to bring justice, to end their ordeal. It had been so long now, all their lives.

'Give us strength for one more day,' they prayed. But when, when O God will it end?

And Jesus said, 'And will not God bring justice for his chosen ones, who cry out to him day and night? Will he keep putting them off? I tell you, he will see that they get justice, and quickly.' O God, when will it end?

JESUS' SALVATION IN HUMAN EXPERIENCE

Christianity is essentially a male dominated religion. Men have set the agenda for the Church for so long that for most Christians a patriarchal Church appears to be the correct expression of Christian life. Women have been reduced to a subordinate role. Women's experience of life and faith is seldom heard in the life of the Church. It is the men who do the speaking, the telling and the interpreting. Women are expected to listen.

Luke gives special emphasis to the role of women in his Gospel narrative, something quite different to the other Gospels. The first two chapters of Luke are dominated by the story of two women, Elizabeth and Mary, and on numerous occasions in his Gospel Luke highlights the way in which Jesus breaks cultural norms which dehumanise and oppress women (Luke 7:36-50; 8:40-56; 10:38-42; 13:10-17; 15:8-10; 21:1-4). But it is in the first two chapters of Luke that we can hear most fully the women's story being told; and it is to these two chapters that we turn to read the story of two women who we've already had occasion to meet, Elizabeth and Mary.

As we turn to their stories our attention will be on the *human* element of the stories rather than on the divine element, for we want to try imaginatively to enter into the experience of Elizabeth and Mary which lies behind Luke's account. As women's stories they are best told by women. At St Philip's the women in the congregation were the major contributors in these two studies. Through their contribution the stories of Elizabeth and Mary became stories of women of flesh and emotion, rather than the romanticised tales we know from Christmas stories.

7. Elizabeth: a Woman's Story of Salvation
Luke 1:1-80 especially verses 5-7, 23-25, 57-58

> 1:5 **In the time of Herod king of Judea, there was a priest named Zechariah, who belonged to the priestly division of Abijah; his**

wife Elizabeth was also a descendant of Aaron. ⁶Both of them were upright in the sight of God, observing all the Lord's commandments and regulations blamelessly. ⁷But they had no children, because Elizabeth was barren; and they were both well on in years.

1:²³When his [Zechariah's] time of service was completed, he returned home. ²⁴After this his wife Elizabeth became pregnant and for five months remained in seclusion. ²⁵'The Lord has done this for me', she said. 'In these days he has shown his favour and taken away my disgrace among the people.'

1:⁵⁷When it was time for Elizabeth to have her baby, she gave birth to a son. ⁵⁸Her neighbours and relatives heard that the Lord had shown her great mercy, and they shared her joy.

Background

The situation of women in the time of Jesus

Women in first century Judaism lived their lives under the control of men, mainly their fathers and their husbands. In Jewish religious and social law, women, slaves and minors were often placed in the same category.

A young girl went through three stages to become a woman. From birth to twelve she was regarded as a small girl. From twelve to twelve-and-a-half she was a young girl, while from twelve-and-a-half onwards she was regarded as a maiden of full age. At marriage she became a woman. The father had full rights over his daughter till she was twelve-and-a-half. This gave him the right to arrange marriage for her and even to sell her into slavery.

The betrothal ceremony, or engagement, was a legal and economic transaction between two families, which began the transfer of the girl from her father's power to her future husband's. Women were usually betrothed between twelve and twelve-and-a-half, often much earlier. A betrothed girl was called a 'wife', could become a widow, be put away by divorce, and be punished by death for adultery. Marriage generally took place one year after betrothal, in a ceremony in which the woman passed finally into the husband's control. The right to divorce was exclusively the husband's.

Barrenness, or infertility, was a tremendously traumatic condition for the woman. It carried immense social stigma; the woman was often reviled and seen as being punished by God. Women who were unable to have children were at the mercy of their husbands, for infertility was sufficient grounds for divorce and the onus for proof of fertility lay with the woman. A husband could take another wife or concubines if his wife proved unsatisfactory.

As the mother of a son, the wife was respected and treasured for she had given her husband the most precious gift of all. While the birth of a son gave great joy, the birth of a daughter was often treated with indifference or sadness.

Further, the worlds of men and women were carefully partitioned off from each other. Publicly, they lived separate lives and had very little in common. Matters of birth and children were almost exclusively the concern of the women. For these reasons we may suppose that the stories of Elizabeth and Mary were preserved and told by the women among the early Christians, for they are essentially women's stories.

Elizabeth's story

The story of Elizabeth is only hinted at in Luke's account. He does not tell her story in any detail, but concentrates, as any male of the first century would, on the story of the birth and naming of a son. Nevertheless Elizabeth remains a key person in the account, for it is she who bears the son; and it is her barrenness that is cured by God.

With the background knowledge we have of the position of women in Jesus' time, let us imagine what Elizabeth's experience of barrenness was like. In the early years of her marriage when she failed to fall pregnant the threat of infertility must have been constantly with her and Zechariah. As the years wore on and it became increasingly clear that they would not have a child, Elizabeth must have endured severe pain in several areas of her life. The most immediate threat would have been that Zechariah would divorce her or marry another woman or even take a concubine. Her relationship with him might well have been very strained at times. Her own family would have been shamed that their daughter could not bear a child; and Zechariah's family may have been very hostile towards her and undermining of their relationship. Imagine Zechariah's parents putting pressure on him to take another wife so that they could have a grandson. In their home village she would have been an object of pity, and sometimes scorn. The women whom she grew up with would have been taken up with their children, and she would have been an awkward participant when they got together around the village well and talked about their babies.

Elizabeth was powerless. She could not change her infertility. Neither could she guarantee her own security. For that she was at the mercy of Zechariah, a man. If he had chosen to do so he could have divorced her, which, if her father refused her refuge with her family, would have had disastrous consequences for her.

Society stamped her as inadequate. She simply did not meet the standards required to be a full and adequate woman. This stigma would have lived with her for all the years of her infertility. The shame of her barrenness was so strong that when in fact she became pregnant late in life, she was still to say, 'The Lord has taken away my disgrace among the people' (Luke 1:25).

And it was to this woman, powerless in a world of men, stigmatised as inadequate, that God's salvation came. He gave her a child, so that she who was shamed carried the one who would announce the coming of God's salvation to the world.

This is the remarkable story of Elizabeth.

Discussion

As we discussed this story at St Philip's it became clear that a number of people, both women and men, had had to face this painful issue of childlessness. Some of the women spoke about the pressures they felt, both within themselves and from others, to have children. Their reactions to these pressures varied. Some thought that they were natural, others thought that such pressures defined women solely in terms of childbearing, which was just a small part of what it was to be a woman. One thing which many women identified with was the experience of often being under the power of men. In this light one of the men spoke about how he had been married to a woman who had had three miscarriages. The stress that this inability to have a child put on her eventually led to a nervous breakdown and permanent hospitalisation in a psychiatric hospital. He recognised the tremendous stress which his wife had been under, and how he too had been part of that stress. His own anguish was clear.

Reflection

The story of Elizabeth is the story of many women; and it touched a deep chord of pain in the lives of some of the women at St Philip's. One woman's story reflected so much of the story of Elizabeth that she too could say, 'The Lord has done this for me. In these days he has taken away my disgrace among people.' God's salvation comes to restore us to the dignity to which we were created. God has wonderfully made us; let God's salvation wonderfully restore us.

Two Songs of Elizabeth

I
I am stubborn ground.
I am a dead bleached tree.
In a field of a hundredfold,
I bear not one thing.

I am a water pot that leaks.
I am rotten and wet wood.
I am a hollow gourd
that makes a gaudy sound.

The satisfied pity me.

You who brought
me forth, be to me seed,
black earth, sweet rain,
that I may call
from my want and warren
your name.

I
I am as sure and as strong as Naomi.
I see angels when I hang out the laundry.
My tongue carves stories
that make the children marvel.

Ho! No man makes me
wonderful. I am wonderfully made.

8. Mary: a Woman's Story of Salvation
Luke 1:26-56; 2:4-7

The story of the birth of Jesus is so well known and has been told so many times that one would think that we know all there is to know about it. But by approaching the story from what was for us a new perspective, we at St Philip's were able to gain some fresh insights into Luke's account of Jesus' birth. We did this by focusing our attention on Mary's experience, and trying to understand what the conception and birth of Jesus meant to her. Mary's story is a woman's story.

1:26In the sixth month, God sent the angel Gabriel to Nazareth, a town in Galilee, 27to a virgin pledged to be married to a man named Joseph, a descendant of David. The virgin's name was Mary. 28The angel went to her and said, 'Greetings, you who are highly favoured! The Lord is with you'. 29Mary was greatly troubled at his words and wondered what kind of greeting this might be. 30But the angel said to her, 'Do not be afraid, Mary, for you have found favour with God. 31You will be with child and give birth to a son, and you are to give him the name Jesus. 32He will be great and called the Son of the Most High. The Lord God will give him the throne of his father David, 33and he will reign over the house of Jacob forever; his kingdom will never end.'

34'How will this be', Mary asked the angel, 'since I am still a virgin'?

35The angel answered, 'The Holy Spirit will come upon you, and the power of the Most High will overshadow you. So the holy one to be born will be called the Son of God. 36Even Elizabeth your relative is going to have a child in her old age, and she who was said to be barren is in her sixth month. 37For nothing is impossible with God.'

38'I am the Lord's servant', Mary answered. 'May it be to me as you have said.' Then the angel left her.

39At that time Mary got ready and hurried to a town in the hill country of Judah, 40where she entered Zechariah's home and greeted Elizabeth. 56Mary stayed with Elizabeth for about three months and then returned home.

2:⁴**So Joseph also went up from the town of Nazareth in Galilee to Judea, to Bethlehem the town of David, because he belonged to the house and line of David. ⁵He went there to be registered with Mary, who was pledged to be married to him and was expecting a child. ⁶While they were there, the time came for the baby to be born, ⁷and she gave birth to her firstborn, a son. She wrapped him in cloths and placed him in a manger, because there was no room for them in the inn.**

Background
The background to this study can be found in the previous study (pp. 56-57).

Mary's story
What image first comes to your mind when you think of Mary, mother of Jesus? Many of us I suppose immediately think of the madonna image, Mary with the baby Jesus in her arms, serene; a woman set apart, who is like no other. Mary has been so romanticised that she is hardly seen as a real person. So let us now, as we did with her cousin Elizabeth, imaginatively enter into her experience.

The first thing we need to realise is that Mary was a young girl, at least by modern western standards, when she was engaged to be married to Joseph. It is likely that she was only twelve years old. We meet Mary on the threshold of puberty, in the delicate period of betrothal when transactions for her marriage to Joseph were being finalised. Suddenly into the life of this ordinary young girl comes an angel who tells her that she is going to become pregnant, not of a man, but from the Holy Spirit of God. Put yourself in Mary's place. What would you have done? Run off to tell your mother, your sister or your best friend? We can guess that if she told anyone they would simply have told her that she was dreaming.

Then she discovers that she is in fact pregnant. It may have taken a little time to discover this, but soon enough it becomes apparent that she is. Imagine the shock this must have been. It was true after all! But how was she to convince her mother that she really did see an angel, that it wasn't all made up, and that she hadn't had sex with anybody. And her father! What was he going to say? After all these careful negotiations for her marriage. And Joseph? Why, he would most probably break off the engagement and his family demand payment to compensate for the embarrassment. (Notice that Luke does not have God speak to Joseph in a dream, telling him that he should marry Mary as Matthew does.) Imagine the anguish this young girl went through.

Pregnant before she was married! The shame of it. What would people think? The scarlet woman, the sinner! What an embarrassment to the families.

So she was packed off to her cousin Elizabeth, way down in the South of Judea. While she was there her fate was no doubt being settled by the respective families back in Galilee. Joseph and his family were in turmoil. So was her family. If Joseph chose to break off the betrothal, she would almost certainly never be able to marry. And if her father chose to throw her out of the house, how would she live? In order to survive, if nobody took her in to their home, she would probably have had to become a prostitute in one of the nearby Greek cities.

Mary's experience was not easy. All she had to sustain her was that one brief encounter with an angel. In the face of the long months of disbelief and the mockery that she had to endure, it was not much to hold on to.

As the nine long months of pregnancy drew to a close Mary was taken off on a long journey down to Bethlehem with Joseph. It was probably a family trip for Joseph's family as they had to go and register at their ancestral home. But Mary was away from her family and in the last days of her pregnancy. In her condition the journey could not have been pleasant. When they eventually arrived in Bethlehem it was teeming with people, filled with large boisterous crowds, and there was no where to stay.

Mary, thirteen years old, her back aching, feeling swollen and heavy, slipped off the donkey and the tears dropped from her eyes. Somehow she knew her time had come. The baby was due, in this strange place, with this strange man who was not yet her husband, and with nowhere to go. At last Joseph came back and said that he had at least found a stable. And there, far from her mother, far from her sisters, far from the midwife who brought her into the world, alone in a stable, Mary went through the frightening, painful, and awesome experience of giving birth.

Reflection

At St Philip's our reflections centred around two things, childbirth and the crisis of unmarried mothers. Some women shared their experience of childbirth; the fears, the pain and the joy that it brought. Frances Bright identified with Mary in a particular way; she too was far away from home and friends when she had her first child; which came after she had been in South Africa for three weeks, having left her family in England. So many years later the anguish of that loneliness was still with her. Some months before, one of the members of our congregation had brought her child to be baptised. She was not married. Our discussion about Mary as an unmarried mother held particular meaning for us as we recognised the immense vulnerability of unmarried mothers in a society like ours. The poem below captures this sense of vulnerability.

Mary

My bosom friend
   steps back into her dark
house as I walk by
(when I am allowed outside at all).
I am a scarlet word in Nazareth,
a wound on my mother's breast
that festers as my body fills.
It was she who said, 'Send her
to Elizabeth until we settle this.'
I am a sullied, sacred cow.
They can't decide
to punish or fear
my power.

We spoke about our church being a place which offered security, acceptance and dignity for women whose dignity had been stripped away; and realised how much a part of society's harsh rejection of them we were. Mary, an unmarried mother, had brought Jesus, God's salvation into the world. This was a great lesson for us to learn.

9. The Rich Ruler: is Jesus' Salvation too Costly?
Luke 18:18-30

We have seen how salvation comes to two women, vulnerable, despised people, who became the bearers of salvation to the world. We now turn to another facet of Luke's portrait of Jesus, where Jesus' salvation is demanding and rigorous and in fact turns people away; it demands considerable sacrifice. Jesus is one who makes radical demands of those who would find salvation through him. Whoever would follow Jesus must first count the cost. They must be like a builder who wants to build a tower, or a king who considers waging war against another; both need to be prepared to pay the cost of the venture. Jesus' disciples may not love their parents, spouses, children, or even themselves more than they love him. Jesus sums all this up: 'Any of you who does not give up everything he has cannot be my disciple' (Luke 14:25-31. See also 9:57-62). In the next two studies we see how Jesus' call to radical discipleship meets with two different responses.

18:¹⁸A certain ruler asked him, 'Good teacher, what must I do to inherit eternal life?'

¹⁹'Why do you call me good?' Jesus answered. 'No-one is good — except God alone. ²⁰You know the commandments: "Do not commit adultery, do not murder, do not steal, do not give false testimony, honour your father and mother."'

²¹'All these I have kept since I was a boy', he said.

²²When Jesus heard this, he said to him, 'You still lack one thing. Sell everything you have and give it to the poor, and you will have treasure in heaven. Then come, follow me'.

²³When he heard this, he became very sad, because he was a man of great wealth. ²⁴Jesus looked at him and said, 'How hard it is for a rich person to enter the kingdom of God! Indeed, it is easier for a camel to go through the eye of a needle than for a rich man to enter the kingdom of God.'

²⁶Those who heard this asked, 'Who then can be saved?'

²⁷Jesus replied. 'What is impossible with men is possible with God.'

²⁸Peter said to him, 'We have left all we had to follow you!'

²⁹'I tell you the truth,' Jesus said to them, 'no-one who has left home or wife or brothers or parents or children for the sake of the

The Rich Ruler: is Jesus' Salvation too Costly? 65

kingdom of God [30]will fail to receive many times as much in this age and, in the age to come, eternal life.'

Notes on the text
18:18   The 'ruler' was most probably a magistrate or member of a regional administrative body. This, combined with his wealth, would have made him a person of power and high social position. We may assume that he was well-educated and aware of the important developments which took place among the lower classes over whom he held authority.

18:21   It appears to have been generally accepted in Jesus' time that it was possible for a person to keep the ten commandments.

18:24   'It is easier for a camel to go through the eye of a needle . . .' is a proverbial expression for something that is impossible. Explanations which suppose the 'eye of a needle' refers to a small gate in the walls of Jerusalem through which a camel could hardly enter, seem to be unfounded. The emphasis is on something which is impossible.

The story of the Rich Ruler
One day a man came up to Jesus and asked him a very important question, a question about eternal life. The man, who was very wealthy and a person of some authority, posed the question in a way which suggests that it was really an academic question. He related to Jesus as a teacher, someone with whom he could have an erudite discussion. Jesus ignored the implicit invitation to a polite discussion and startled the man by asking him why he addressed him as 'good teacher'. This had the effect of making the conversation an intimate personal encounter. Jesus engaged the man on a personal level. The possibility of a dispassionate academic conversation was lost. Without waiting for a reply to his question, Jesus listed a number of the ten commandments with the implication that it was by following the commandments that one found eternal life. This is at least what the ruler understood him to mean, for he replied that he had kept them all since he was a boy. His reply was probably sincere, for he could claim with some legitimacy that he had neither murdered, committed adultery or transgressed any of the other commandments Jesus listed.

Jesus did not dispute his claim. But he drove home to the heart of what he saw this man's problem to be — his wealth. Jesus made it quite clear that if this man was to find salvation he had first to sell all he had and then become one of his disciples. Here was a person who had wealth, status and power, yet Jesus' reply made him sad for it demanded of him that he relinquish all these things. Jesus accepted no other way.

Discussion

In our discussion at St Philip's we felt that one of the central features of Luke's account of the encounter between Jesus and the ruler was something that was silent in the text. For we noticed that Jesus' list of commandments in 18:20 omitted the first four commandments, which Jewish law of the time summarised as 'Love the Lord your God with all your heart and with all your soul and with all your mind and love your neighbour as yourself.' It became clear to us that when Jesus asked the rich ruler to sell all he had, he was in fact testing his love for God and his love for his neighbour. Clearly, wealth and the prestige it brought him were obstacles to this man truly loving God and his fellow people. He could not obey the first commandment while he was wealthy.

We noticed too that Jesus then made a statement which applied the problem this individual faced to rich people in general. 'How hard it is for the rich to enter the kingdom of God!' said Jesus (Luke 18:24). This led us onto a discussion about whether one could be rich and still be a Christian. We first noticed that Jesus said that all things are possible to God, but that he made it very clear that wealth and power were in conflict with his salvation for they inhibited one's ability to truly love God and one's neighbour.

Reflection

Our initial response to this story was to ask ourselves if there was anything which came between us and our following of Christ. Were there things in our lives which prevented us from loving God with all our heart, soul, mind and strength, and our neighbours as ourselves? We spent some time talking about this important and searching question. Then someone suggested that a general discussion like this was good and fruitful, but it was not a direct response to the story of the rich man and Jesus. There the specific issue that kept the man from loving God and his neighbour was wealth. This was the issue that

The Rich Ruler: is Jesus' Salvation too Costly?

Jesus addressed. In the ensuing heated discussion such questions as 'Who is to be defined as wealthy?', 'Does Jesus really require us to sell all we have and give to the poor?', 'Are we not meant to be good stewards of our wealth?' were raised without reaching any consensus. We wryly concluded that the question of wealth tested our commitment to the Gospel more radically than we might have anticipated. Finally, we prayerfully read other passages in Luke which spoke about wealth. Here, those passages are given in the form of a responsive reading.

A responsive reading of texts from Luke on the theme of wealth

Unison   Your word, O God, created the world and sustains the universe. Grant that by the work of the Holy Spirit we may hear that word and be recreated by it. Enable us to respond willingly to Jesus' call to a radical discipleship.

Group A   God has brought down rulers from their thrones but has lifted up the humble. He has filled the hungry with good things but has sent the rich away empty. (1:52-53)

Group B   Looking at his disciples, Jesus said:
'Blessed are you who are poor
   for yours is the kingdom of God.
Blessed are you who hunger now,
   for you will be satisfied.' (6:20-21)

Group A   And he went on to say:
'But woe to you who are rich,
   for you have already received your comfort.
Woe to you who are well fed now,
   for you will go hungry.' (6:24-25)

Group B   Jesus also said:
'If anyone would come after me, he must take up his cross daily and follow me. For whoever wants to save his life will lose it and whoever loses his life for me will save it. What good is it for a man to gain the whole world, and yet lose or forfeit his very self?' (9:23-25)

Group A   He also said:
'Sell your possessions and give to the poor. Provide purses

for yourselves that will not wear out, a treasure in heaven that will not be exhausted, where no thief comes near and no moth destroys. For where your treasure is, there your heart will be also.'   (12:33-34)

Group B Jesus told his disciples:
'No servant can serve two masters. Either he will hate the one and love the other, or he will be devoted to the one and despise the other. You cannot serve both God and Money.'   (16:13)

Pause for reflection

Group A And he told them this parable:

All The ground of a certain rich man produced a good crop. He thought to himself, 'What shall I do? I have no place to store my crops.' Then he said, 'This is what I'll do. I will tear down my barns and build bigger ones, and then I will store all my grain and my goods. And I'll say to myself, "You have plenty of good things laid up for many years. Take life easy; eat, drink and be merry."'

Group A But God said to him, 'You fool! This very night your life will be demanded from you. Then what have you prepared for yourself?' This is how it will be with anyone who stores up things for himself but is not rich towards God. (12:16-21)

Group A Then Jesus said to his host,

All 'When you give a luncheon or dinner, do not invite your friends, your brothers or relatives, or your rich neighbours; if you do, they may invite you back and so you will be repaid. But when you give a banquet, invite the poor, the crippled, the lame, the blind, and you will be blessed.' (14:12-14)

Paraphrase of Luke 16:19-31

There was an affluent Capetonian who drove a Mercedes Benz, ate well every day and lived in a large house in Rondebosch. Often a woman from Khayelitsha named Thembeka would come and beg at his backdoor. Thembeka would see the food, the clothes, and the warmth of the house and longed that she might have but a small portion of it. Only the dogs befriended her.

One day Thembeka died of pneumonia during the cold wet winter. She went to heaven. The rich man also died, only he went to hell. In his torment he looked up towards heaven and saw Abraham holding Thembeka, and he asked Abraham for something to drink. But Abraham said, 'You in your lifetime were comfortable while this person suffered; but now she is comforted and you are in anguish.' Then the rich man asked Abraham to send Thembeka to his family and to his church in Kenilworth so that they would not also go to hell. But Abraham replied, 'They have the scriptures; let them hear them.' And the rich man said: 'No Abraham; if someone goes to them from the dead they will repent.' But Abraham said, 'If they do not hear the teaching of Moses and the prophets, of Jesus and Paul, neither will they be convinced if someone should raise them from the dead.'

[Rondebosch and Kenilworth are affluent white suburbs of Cape Town. Khayelitsha is a vast desolate Black township built on sand dunes outside the city. Tens of thousands of people live there under extremely poor conditions. A high proportion of them are unemployed.]

10. Zacchaeus: Jesus' Salvation is Not too Costly!
Luke 19:1-10

The inclination for human beings to make heroes of people appears to be a universal human trait. No culture is without its heroes, its celebrities, its honoured and revered members. Heroes embody or achieve those things most highly prized in a society. Ordinary people see in them virtues which they themselves desire. That heroes come in all shapes and sizes simply reflects that human society has vastly differing values. And so we find military heroes and pacifist heroes, religious saints and movie stars, Ghandi and Jinnah, Beethoven and the Beatles, Idi Amin and Jomo Kenyatta. The list could go on and on. These heroes reflect some of the dominant values of the societies that make them the celebrities they are.

Zacchaeus: Jesus' Salvation is Not too Costly!

South Africa has no lack of heroes; but it is a nation with no shared heroes, for its heroes represent its divisions. This is one of the tragedies of this land. Black soccer stars versus white rugby stars; the Mandelas, Tambos, Bikos versus the Verwoeds, Malans and Bothas; the Buthelezis and Matanzimas versus the Sisulus and the Gumedes of the UDF. This list could go on an on. However, there is one hero that could at least claim to have followers in most segments of the country. But then this hero is found in all countries influenced by western culture. This hero is one of the most enduring and powerful heroes of the past two centuries: the person who grows up poor and makes their fortune; the impoverished American immigrant who in the land of opportunity makes his first million by the time he is thirty. The rags to riches hero. The hero of the great American dream. The immigrant-hero has now matured into the tycoon-hero who ruthlessly treads over everyone who gets in the way of making millions. The J.R. Ewing hero. This hero is a product of a society which believes that wealth is the ultimate goal of life, and that all things are permissible in the pursuit of it. What a hero!

In Luke's Gospel we find a completely different hero. A completely different success story. It is the story of a rich person who sells all he has and gives to the poor and to those whom he has cheated. Zacchaeus is this most unlikely hero.

> 19:[1] Jesus entered Jericho and was passing through. [2] A man was there by the name of Zacchaeus; he was a chief tax collector and was wealthy. [3] He wanted to see who Jesus was, but being a short man he could not, because of the crowd. [4] So he ran ahead and climbed a sycamore-fig tree to see him, since Jesus was coming that way.
>
> [5] When Jesus reached the spot, he looked up and said to him, 'Zacchaeus, come down immediately. I must stay at your house today.' [6] So he came down at once and welcomed him gladly.
>
> [7] All the people saw this and began to mutter, 'He has gone to be the guest of a "sinner".'
>
> [8] But Zacchaeus stood up and said to the Lord, 'Look, Lord! Here and now I give half my possessions to the poor, and if I have cheated anybody out of anything, I will pay back four times the amount.'
>
> [9] Jesus said to him, 'Today salvation has come to this house, because this man, too, is a son of Abraham. [10] For the Son of Man came to seek and to save what was lost.'

Zacchaeus: Jesus' Salvation is Not too Costly!

Other texts to read
Luke 3:12-13; 5:27-32; 15:1; 18:9-14

Notes on the text
19:1 Jericho was the second largest city in Judea, to the east of Jerusalem. (See the map on page 00.) It was a large trade centre as it lay on the major caravan route from the East to Judea and Jerusalem. It also dominated the southern stretch of the Jordan valley with its large estates owned by the Roman emperor.

19:2 The *New International Version* says that Zacchaeus was a chief tax collector. The Greek is best translated 'chief *toll* collector'. Toll collecting — the collection of indirect taxes such as tolls, tariffs and customs duties — was part of the lucrative business of tax farming. The Roman authorities used private individuals to collect their taxes for them. The collection of taxes was auctioned off to the highest bidder who became the chief toll collector, and he in turn sub-contracted out various aspects of toll collection to other individuals. Three features of this institution are important for our purposes. Firstly, tax and toll collectors were notoriously corrupt. Since the chief collector had to pay the expected revenue to the Romans in advance and then recover the amount, plus expenses and profit, by setting the amount of the tolls and then collecting them, the abuse of their powers was rife. This made them most unpopular figures. Secondly, these toll collectors were employees and agents of the Roman empire; participating in the execution of an abhorred practice, collecting taxes for the oppressor. For a Jew to do this to another was loathesome. Toll collectors were not popular people in Galilee and Judea. They were shunned and ostracised in Jewish society. Notice how, in verse 7, when Jesus goes to Zacchaeus's house the people protest saying that he has gone to the house of a sinner. The word sinner, *hamartolos*, was also a favourite word for 'heathen', who were shunned. Thirdly, tax collectors were considered to be ritually unclean by the religious establishment of the day. This was because they had to engage in business transactions with Gentiles; something which made them religiously unclean.

Discussion
The early readers of Luke's Gospel would have been familiar with such tax collectors. They were to be found all over the Roman empire.

72 Zacchaeus: Jesus' Salvation is Not too Costly!

This might well have been in the back of Luke's mind as he wrote his Gospel, for one of the features which distinguishes Luke from the other Gospels is the way in which Jesus' relationship with tax collectors is developed; for example, the story of Zacchaeus is found only in Luke. It is also consistent with Luke's portrait of Jesus as the one who has come not to call the righteous and the powerful but sinners and those who are weak.

Tax collectors feature in the Lukan narrative from before Jesus' baptism. They came to John the Baptist to be baptised with the baptism of repentance, and they asked him what they should do. He replied, 'Don't collect any more than you are required to' (Luke 3:12-13). Very early on in his ministry Jesus called his disciples, among whom was Levi (Matthew). Levi was a tax collector. When Jesus saw him he said, 'Follow me'. Levi got up, and significantly for Luke, left everything and followed Jesus. As a farewell fling, Levi threw a party for his ex-colleagues. A large crowd of them attended, as did Jesus. And the Pharisees, whose name means 'the separated ones', were dismayed by the way in which Jesus associated with these religious outcasts (Luke 5:27-32). Jesus becomes known as 'the friend of tax collectors and "sinners"' (7:34) and it is they who gather around him (15:1) when he teaches.

It is only Luke who records the parable of the Pharisee and the tax collector who go into the temple to pray (18:9-14). The Pharisee prays a self-righteous prayer, thanking God that he is not a sinner like the tax collector. In contrast, the tax collector asks God for mercy for he is a sinner. It is he who goes home justified before God. The familiar theme in Luke that the proud will be humbled and the humble will be exalted emerges once again.

By the time Jesus reached Jericho on his journey to Jerusalem (see study 11 for details of this journey) he was guaranteed to collect a crowd around him, for wherever he went people were eager to see this miracle-working teacher. And since he was called the friend of tax collectors, it is no surprise to find the diminutive chief tax collector of Jericho scurrying up a tree to see this compelling person as he passed through town. And it is this tax collector who is the unlikely hero of Luke's Gospel. His response to Jesus is not sadness, like the rich ruler, but gladness. And with no prompting that we know of Zacchaeus demonstrates that he indeed loves God and his neighbours, for he gives half his wealth to the poor and reimburses those whom he has defrauded four times the amount he cheated them.

Here is the true Lukan hero; the one who gives away his wealth that he might find salvation. And Jesus pronounces that salvation: 'Today salvation has come to this house, because this man, too, is a son of Abraham.' The thief has made restoration; the oppressor has ceased his oppression; the hated one is now loved; the outcast restored to fellowship; the wealthy one has now become poor; and the sinner is forgiven. Salvation is not too costly!

Reflection
The story below, which aptly captures the essence of Zacchaeus' story, was told during our reflection on the text.

Zacchaeus in Cape Town, August 1986
One winter Saturday afternoon Jesus passed through Guguletu. His eventual destination was the houses of Parliament and the NGK synod hall in Wale Street, where he would have a final showdown with the political and religious authorities before being put to death. But this was far from the minds of the excited people as they milled around in the crowd that accompanied Jesus through the township. The warm sunlight was a respite from the week of cold and bitter rain; already the large pools of water in the roads and outside the houses were mere puddles. There was a buoyancy in the air, almost a carnival spirit. Even the boere were absent; their lethal presence in their casspirs and buffels, with their guns and teargas was not missed, yet they were not forgotten. You forgot them at your peril. Few people expected to enjoy being part of a vibrant, festive crowd for long before the boere came and disrupted this illegal gathering.

But enjoy it they would! 'Why this Jesus! Hey man he's great. Doesn't give a damn about the government. The things he was saying last week in Zwelitsha. This government are going to get him for sure!' 'I wonder if he's going to do something today? I wouldn't mind something to eat. Hey, wait. Ssht. He's stopped. Right there under that bluegum tree. Who's he talking to? What?!! Zac Zakhile, the community councillor?'

Suddenly there was a tense silence. Jesus' words could be clearly heard. 'Zakhile, come down immediately, I must stay at your house today.' The silence lasted a few more strained moments. Zakhile was seen slithering down the tree. As he touched ground the shout 'Impimpi! Impimpi! Necklace him!' electrified the crowd. They surged forward. But in that moment between thought and action their attention was captured.

Zakhile was speaking. That loud, hated, overbearing voice of his had changed. That was what gripped them. Somehow his words were touching them. And as he spoke to Jesus, telling him that he saw that what he had been doing was so bitterly wrong, the crowd hung on his words. 'Yes,' he said, 'I will give half of what I own to the poor. I have extorted money; to those people I will repay four times as much as I took. I resign from my job. I will take down the security fence from around my house. I will welcome guests. My daughters will be called back home from where I sent them for safety. I will go to my son in detention the first visit I can get. To him I will say that I am sorry.'

And Jesus said, 'Today salvation has come to this man and his house.'

Explanatory notes: Gugguletu is a large Black township in Cape Town. The *NGK* (Nederduitse Gereformeerde Kerk) is the dominant Afrikaans church in South Africa which has consistently given the Apartheid government its full legitimation over the passed forty years. *Boere:* a slang term for the police and army. *Casspirs and buffels:* armoured troop carriers which continuously patrol the Black townships. *Zwelitsha:* a turbulent township some ninety kilometres from Cape Town. *Community councillors:* Blacks who serve on government appointed boards. They, like the tax collectors, are hated as collaborators with the oppressors. They have been the focus of violent attacks. *Impimpi:* Collaborator, traitor. *Necklace:* to put someone to death by tying them up and then placing a motorcar tyre around their neck and setting it alight.

JERUSALEM: THE DESTINY OF GOD'S SALVATION

Jerusalem is the city of destiny. The narrative of Luke's Gospel builds up to the point where Jesus finally reaches his destination: Jerusalem. Luke, like no other Gospel, is preoccupied with Jerusalem as the city of destiny for Jesus. Jerusalem frames the Gospel narrative; it opens with Zechariah in the temple in Jerusalem (Luke 1:8) and it ends with Jesus commanding the disciples to remain in the city and wait to be clothed with power from God (Luke 24:49). And after the ascension, 'they worshipped him and returned to Jerusalem with great joy, and they stayed continually at the temple, praising God' (Luke 24:52-53). Jerusalem is the primary geographic reference in the Gospel; only the sections on John the Baptist and Jesus (Luke 3:1-4:13), and the period of Jesus' ministry in Galilee (4:14-9:50) are not dominated by the city.

As a small baby Jesus is taken to Jerusalem to be presented in the temple (Luke 2:21-40). The only childhood account we have of Jesus in the Gospels is found in Luke: the story of Jesus' visit to Jerusalem with his parents for the Passover (Luke 2:41-52). Jerusalem does not figure in Jesus' early ministry which takes place in Galilee; but it re-enters the gospel story in Luke 9:51 when Jesus begins a journey towards Jerusalem which frames the rest of his public ministry before he enters Jerusalem (Luke 9:51-19:27). The last five chapters of Luke are set in Jerusalem, where Jesus is in open conflict with the powerful rulers of the Jews; a conflict which culminates in his trial and death in the city. The pivotal role of the city is again emphasised in Luke 24; the risen Jesus appears only in the vicinity of Jerusalem. Luke does not include an account of Jesus' appearances in Galilee, as do Matthew (28:7,16-18) and John (21:1-14). Jesus' ascension takes place in Bethany, just outside Jerusalem; immediately after which the disciples return to Jerusalem and there await the coming of God's power. Jerusalem is the city of destiny.

Geography, therefore, is an important element of Luke's portrait of Jesus. The revelation of Jesus' salvation is demarcated by geography. It is first known in Jerusalem, then in Galilee; but soon it proceeds relentlessly back to Jerusalem where it meets its final destiny. Luke's concern with geography is continued in his second volume, Acts, which opens with the disciples waiting in Jerusalem to receive the Holy Spirit (1:4-5) and with Jesus' words 'But you will receive power when the Holy Spirit comes upon you; and you will be my witnesses in Jerusalem, and in all Judea and Samaria, and to the ends of the earth' (1:8). The rest of the book of Acts is the story of how the Church, starting in Jerusalem, spread its influence all the way to Rome, the capital city of the empire. The journey motif is dominant in Acts.

The last three Bible studies centre on Jerusalem: Jesus' journey to Jerusalem and what takes place in the city of destiny, Jesus' death and his resurrection. The first of these studies focuses on Jesus as he journeys to his destiny.

11. Jerusalem: Jesus Journeys to his Destiny
Luke 9:30-31,51-53,56; 13:22,31-35; 17:11; 18:31-33; 19:1,11,28-29,41

9:³⁰Two men, Moses and Elijah, ³¹appeared in glorious splendour, talking with Jesus. They spoke about his departure, which he was about to bring to fulfilment at Jerusalem.

9:⁵¹As the time approached for him to be taken up to heaven, Jesus resolutely set out for Jerusalem, ⁵²and he sent messengers on ahead. They went into a Samaritan village to get things ready for him, ⁵³but the people there did not welcome him, because he was heading for Jerusalem . . . ⁵⁶and they went to another village.

13:²²Then Jesus went through the towns and villages, teaching as he made his way to Jerusalem.

13:³¹At the same time some Pharisees came to Jesus and said to him, 'Leave this place and go somewhere else. Herod wants to kill you.' ³²He replied, 'Go tell that fox, "I will drive out demons and heal people today and tomorrow, and on the third day I will reach my goal." ³³In any case, I must keep going today and tomorrow and the next day — for surely no prophet can die outside of Jerusalem! ³⁴O Jerusalem, Jerusalem, you who kill the prophets and stone those sent to you, how often I have longed to gather your children

Jerusalem: Jesus Journeys to his Destiny

together, as a hen gathers her chicks under her wings, but you were not willing!'

17:¹¹Now on his way to Jerusalem, Jesus travelled along the border between Samaria and Galilee.

18:³¹Jesus took the Twelve aside and told them, 'We are going up to Jerusalem, and everything that is written by the prophets about the Son of Man will be fulfilled. ³²He will be turned over to the Gentiles. They will mock him, insult him, spit on him, flog him, and kill him. ³³On the third day he will rise again.

19:¹Jesus entered Jericho and was passing through. ¹¹While they were listening to this, he went on to tell them a parable, because he was near to Jerusalem. ²⁸After Jesus had said this, he went on ahead, going up to Jerusalem. ²⁹As he approached Bethpage and Bethany at the hill called the Mount of Olives. . . .

19:⁴¹As he approached Jerusalem and saw the city, he wept over it. . . .

Notes on the texts

9:30-31   For Luke the climax of Jesus' ministry in Galilee is the transfiguration. Shortly after this Jesus begins his journey to Jerusalem. Luke alone indicates what Moses, Elijah and Jesus spoke about: Jesus' departure from this world, the ascension which would take place in Jerusalem after his death and resurrection. At the focal point of Jesus' ministry in Galilee the focus of the Gospel shifts to Jerusalem.

9:51-56   This is another reference to the ascension. The key phrase here is, 'Jesus resolutely set out for Jerusalem'. There is a clear sense of purpose and determination in Luke's portrait of Jesus. He is the one who 'sets his face toward Jerusalem' (RSV); he knows that Jerusalem is the city of his destiny.

The Samaritans had for centuries had a hostile relationship with the Jews. When they broke from the Jews is not clear, but we know that they established a rival temple to Jerusalem on Mount Gerazim and only accepted the first five books of the Old Testament. They occupied the territory between Galilee in the North and Judea in the South, with their capital at Samaria or Sebaste. Their hostility to Jesus may stem from the fact that he was going to Jerusalem. Apparently, Jewish pilgrims on their way to Jerusalem often experienced

Jerusalem: Jesus Journeys to his Destiny

JESUS' JOURNEY TO JERUSALEM

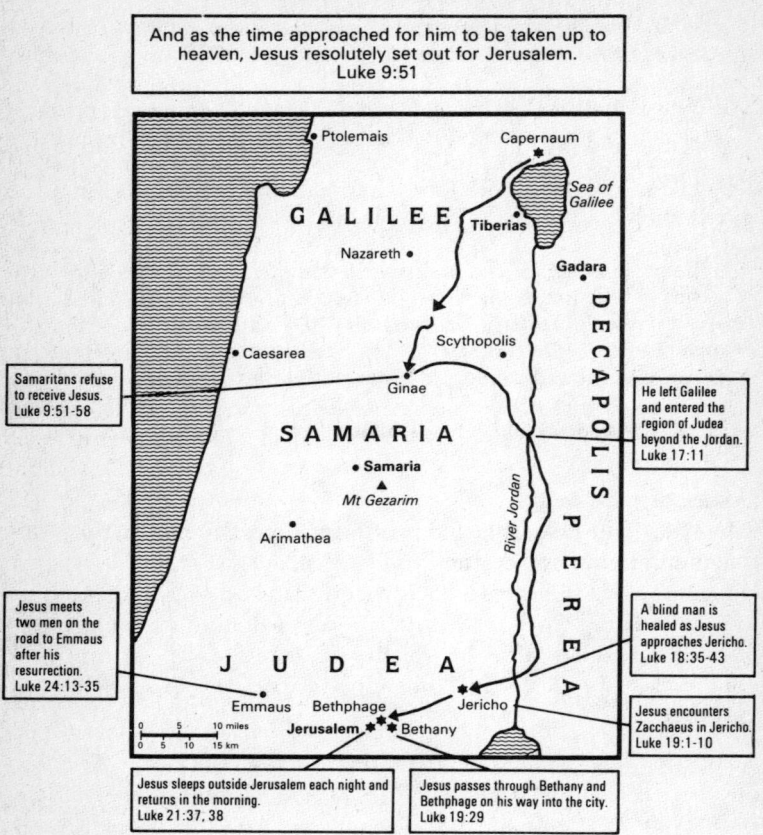

> And as the time approached for him to be taken up to heaven, Jesus resolutely set out for Jerusalem.
> Luke 9:51

Samaritans refuse to receive Jesus. Luke 9:51-58

He left Galilee and entered the region of Judea beyond the Jordan. Luke 17:11

Jesus meets two men on the road to Emmaus after his resurrection. Luke 24:13-35

A blind man is healed as Jesus approaches Jericho. Luke 18:35-43

Jesus encounters Zacchaeus in Jericho. Luke 19:1-10

Jesus sleeps outside Jerusalem each night and returns in the morning. Luke 21:37, 38

Jesus passes through Bethany and Bethphage on his way into the city. Luke 19:29

difficulties in Samaria; the Samaritans resented people who travelled through their country on their way to Jerusalem, the rival temple-city to Mt Gezarim. The normal route to Jerusalem from Galilee, which Jesus took, crossed over the river Jordan into Perea in order to avoid Samaria, and then recrossed the Jordan east of Jericho. (See the map on Jesus' journey, above.) Jesus rejects his disciples' suggestion that the Samaritans be punished for their response. The other two times the Samaritans are mentioned in the Gospel they appear in a good light: the parable of the good Samaritan (Luke

Jerusalem: Jesus Journeys to his Destiny

10:25-37), and the Samaritan leper who was the only one out of ten whom Jesus healed to return to thank Jesus (17:11-19).

13:22 The actual progress of the journey is sluggish. Jesus and his disciples meander through the country while Jesus teaches and heals in the villages and towns they go through. The sense of a journey is often lost in Luke's narrative, as the travel accounts are brief and scattered whilst Jesus' teaching and healing activity dominates the story.

13:31-35 Notice that some Pharisees side with Jesus against Herod Antipas. Not all Pharisees, by any means, were the hypocrites they are sometimes depicted to be. It was Herod Antipas who had John the Baptist beheaded; now he seeks to kill Jesus. Luke constantly presents Jesus' salvation as a costly salvation. John the Baptist died, and indeed Jesus himself suffered the threat of death from a ruler who felt threatened by his message. Jesus does not flee death, but goes on to the city of destiny, Jerusalem. His journey must not flag. He will die in Jerusalem. It will not be Herod who kills him but those who rule Jerusalem, for Jerusalem is where prophets die. As a prophet it is Jesus' destiny to die in Jerusalem. Verses 31 to 33 are unique to Luke.

And as a prophet Jesus weeps over Jerusalem. In one of the most tender images in the Gospel Jesus grieves over Jerusalem; picturing himself as a hen protecting her chicks under her wing, bringing to Jerusalem her salvation. Jesus' salvation comes with all the tenderness of a mother protecting her offspring. But the rulers of Jerusalem reject this salvation!

The journey goes on (17:11). Sometime before they reach Jericho Jesus takes the twelve disciples aside and warns them what his destiny in Jerusalem is to be. He will be given over to the gentiles, mocked and tortured and killed by them. But, on the third day, he will rise again (18:31-33).

The references to the journey to Jerusalem increase as Jesus and his disciples get nearer the city. The momentum picks up as Luke artfully creates a sense of intense expectation (18:31-33; 19:1,11,28,29,41) which culminates in Jesus' heralded entry into the city (19:32-39).

80   Jerusalem: Jesus Journeys to his Destiny

Discussion
The journey has immense significance for Luke's portrait of Jesus because it shows Jesus as one who knew with certainty what his destiny was and where it lay. He was not a confused individual to whom history was happening beyond his control. Jesus was able to control what happened to him because he knew what he had come to earth to do: go to Jerusalem to die. Jesus is the one who is in authority.

On this slow and much interrupted journey Jesus trains his disciples. He equips his Galilean followers, who are now out of their home territory, for the mission of proclaiming him and his message of salvation after his death and resurrection. Soon, after the coming of the Holy Spirit, the young Church would be announcing the good news of Jesus Christ in a foreign and often hostile world. For Luke's readers this journey, this section of Luke's story, is a training manual for them too; for in it they can see how Jesus himself went on a missionary journey, and how he trained his disciples to do so as well. (See especially Luke 10:1-24.)

Reflection
In our reflection on the passage we equated Jerusalem with Johannesburg. Just as Jerusalem was the economic and political centre of Judea, so Johannesburg, with the largest concentration of wealth and industry and the politically potent Soweto and Pretoria nearby, is the power centre of South Africa. Jesus' mission was to go to Jerusalem, the city of destiny, and there confront the ruling class. Johannesburg is seen by many as the city of destiny for South Africa; for it is in this complex of cities that South Africa's future will be worked out. As individuals we felt that there was little we could do about matters on such a large scale; but believed that the Church, as a body, could have great effect in the Johannesburg arena.

We felt, however, that we could not escape our responsibility to find our Jerusalem; the point where we were to challenge the ruling class ourselves. We felt that too often as Christians we view the final destination of our journey, heaven, as the only really important thing in our lives. We often live on earth with no real sense of purpose or calling for our lives in the hard political world. St Philip's, we felt, was increasingly coming to understand what its Jerusalem was; its destiny in the South African turmoil. The journey to Jerusalem had begun.

The Journey
*(a poem inspired by Cavafy's 'Ithaka'
and the Gospel of Luke)*

When you set out for Jerusalem
ask that your way be long,
full of instruction, full of labour.
At many a summer dawn to begin
— with what expectation, what tenacity —
a new day filled with rich purpose;
to live as Christ has called.
To be like Zacchaeus, his riches given away,
'Salvation has come to this house this day!'
To be as the leper was; one out of ten,
his gratitude he brought, outcast Samaritan he.
To go out as they were sent;
good news to the poor, release to the captive,
sight to the blind.

The magistrates and the soldiers,
angry rulers — do not fear them.
Such as these will never kill your soul.
Gather the strength this knowledge brings;
speak straight words of truth; strong words of justice.
Hated; you will be blessed.
Scorned, excluded, reviled; you as he.

When you set out for Jerusalem
ask that your way be long;
but have Jerusalem always on your mind.
Your arrival there is what you are destined for.

12. Jerusalem: Jesus' Salvation in Conflict with the Powerful

Luke 19:45-48; 20:19-20; 20:45-21:6; 21:37-38; 22:1-6; 22:47-53; 22:66-23:5; 23:13-25

Jerusalem is not Johannesburg but Umtata! In the previous study I suggested that Jerusalem should be equated with Johannesburg. This is a helpful analogy; but if we step back and view Jerusalem in the light of the vast Roman empire, a different picture emerges. From that perspective Jerusalem shrinks to a small regional centre, whose political rulers wield little influence in the outside world, and whose ruling class collaborates extensively with the overlords, the Romans. They are insecure, easily threatened and quick to react to protect their own interests.

The parallel to this Jerusalem in South Africa is Umtata, capital city of the Republic of the Transkei (or any other of the homeland capitals). Umtata is a capital city only in name; no country recognises its sovereignty other than its creator, South Africa. Its ruling class is insecure; collaborators with the grand scheme of apartheid, they face massive opposition. In fear, they strike out viciously to protect themselves. Transkeian security police out-brutalise South African police. If Jesus was born in South Africa today, he might well be born in a rural village in the hill country of the Transkei and die in a prison in Umtata.

Jerusalem is the place of conflict in Luke's Gospel. Jesus was locked in conflict from the moment he entered Jerusalem; his adversaries, 'the chief priests, the teachers of the law and the leaders of the people', were the ruling class in Jerusalem. This conflict culminates in Jesus' death; a death clearly sought for and secured by the Jerusalem authorities. Our focus in this study will be on Jesus' opponents in Jerusalem. Why did they want him crucified? What threat did he pose to them? Luke has a very clear understanding about these questions, and it will be our object to discover how he understood Jesus' death.

Background: the ruling class and the Jerusalem temple

Who constituted the ruling class with whom Jesus was locked in conflict? Luke repeatedly uses the phrase 'chief priests, teachers of the law and the elders among the people' or a variation of it (19:47; 20:1,19; 22:2,52,66; 23:13) to describe them, and he uses the phrase only once Jesus has entered Jerusalem. These people, all men, represent the civil and religious authority in Jerusalem. There was a two-tier structure of authority in the city: the upper tier being the Roman imperial authority. Judea had lost any form of political autonomy (which Galilee still to some extent enjoyed under King Herod Antipas) and was ruled by a Roman procurator. The procurator did not live in Jerusalem, but he made regular visits to it; the Roman army maintained a constant presence in the city. His primary concern was keeping the peace and ensuring the efficient flow of taxes to Rome. Pontius Pilate was procurator when Jesus entered Jerusalem. The rest of Judean life, religious, civil and what political life was left, was the responsibility of the second tier of the Jerusalem authorities; the chief priests, scribes (teachers of the law) and elders whose authority lay in the Sanhedrin or 'council of the elders' as Luke calls it (22:66).

Day-to-day legislation of Jewish affairs was in the hands of this body of seventy-two men who represented the aristocracy of Jerusalem; the wealthy elite whose power touched every aspect of Jewish life. All matters religious and civil came under their authority; there was no separation of religious and secular authority. The high priest presided over the Sanhedrin. Appointed by the Romans, the high priests and their families were vested with considerable powers and prestige. Caiaphas (whom Luke mentions only in 3:2) was high priest at the time of the conflict with Jesus. The majority of the ruling class belonged by birth to the influential Sadducees, an urban elite who were large land owners.

The continued status of these people, both in terms of their authority and their wealth, rested primarily on two things: first, their good standing with the Romans; second, their continued control of the temple in Jerusalem. Roman rule was clear on what it wanted from its subjects: a peaceful existence — revolts were expensive things and required troops which would be better deployed on the empire's borders than on internal revolts — and a goodly haul of taxes to keep the empire splendid and its aristocracy wealthy. Local rulers who were not able to keep their people peaceful were quickly replaced and often put to death. The ruling class knew this very well. They had seen it happen often in their turbulent city. Rabble-rousers were the very worst kind of people to them; they initiated riots and too many riots led to a change in the Jerusalem elite. Their authority over the populace of Jerusalem was central to them being able to ensure the peace Rome required. They collaborated with the Romans as best they could.

As we noticed in the introduction, Judea did not have a strong economy. The fact that there could exist in such a region a city as large as Jerusalem was anomalous, for Judea was far too poor to provide an economy that could sustain it. The key to Jerusalem's ability to survive lay in the remarkable ability of the temple to generate wealth and economic activity; and the ruling class controlled the temple.

The temple was the focus of religious attention for hundreds of thousands of Jews from all over the Roman empire and beyond. Jews from Alexandria in North Africa, to Rome in Italy and Babylon in Mesopotamia recognised it as the central shrine of their faith (see Acts 2:5-12 for Luke's list of foreigners in Jerusalem) the place where once a year the high priest entered the most holy place and offered sacrifices on behalf of the Jewish people. To this temple came thousands of Jews on pilgrimage each year, ready to offer their sacrifices and participate in the religious festivals, the biggest and best attended of which was the Passover. Luke tells us that after Jesus' birth Mary and Joseph went down to Jerusalem and offered the required sacrifice following Jesus' dedication (Luke 2:22-24). It was also their custom each year to go to Jerusalem for the Passover festival (Luke 2:41,42). Such pilgrims as Mary and Joseph were the economic life-blood of Jerusalem. They brought huge revenues to the temple's coffers; changing their currency into special temple currency (always a lucrative business for the money changers), buying animals for sacrifice (the flesh of which was eaten by the priests), giving offerings such as money, parcels of land or houses (which would then become the property of the temple priests) and renting board and lodging in the city. The pilgrims brought in substantial moneys.

There was a second and equally important source of revenue which the temple brought in: the temple tax, which was required of every male Jew regardless of where he lived. (See Matthew 17:24-27.) This tax was intended for the maintenance of public worship and was

Jerusalem: Jesus' Salvation in Conflict with the Powerful

used to ensure the efficient running of the temple. It was a major source of revenue for the temple; enabling massive building projects and the most beautiful furnishings and decorations. The building programme which began under Herod the Great lasted till 63 CE; at its height it employed over 18,000 people. Josephus, a Jewish historian who saw the temple after it was completed, wrote this of it:

> The exterior of the structure lacked nothing that could astound either mind or eye. For, being covered on all sides with massive plates of gold, the sun was no sooner upon it than it radiated so fiery a flash that people straining to look at it were compelled to avert their eyes, as from the rays of the sun. To approaching strangers it appeared from afar like a snow-clad mountain; for all that was not overlaid with gold was of the purest white. From its summit protruded sharp golden spikes to prevent birds from settling upon and befouling the roof. Some of the stones in the structure were forty-five cubits in length, five in height, and six in breadth. (*The Jewish Wars* 5.5,6 22-24.)

Not only were builders employed by the temple but scores of others trades served it too; candle makers, herders for the temple flocks, incense dealers, plumbers and bakers — the list goes on.

The main way in which the ruling class ensured its success in keeping the peace in Jerusalem and in ensuring a continual supply of money to the temple, was by means of its control of Jewish religion. In tandem with the Romans, the ruling class in Jerusalem taxed the lower classes to the point of ruin. Religion was used to ensure the comfort of the elite at the expense of the peasantry of Palestine.

In this study we will be dealing with a large group of texts. The intention is not to deal with each text in detail but to get the sense of the dynamics between Jesus and the ruling class. You may find it helpful to read all of 19:28-23:56.

> **19:**[45]**Then he entered the temple area and began driving out those who were selling.** [46]**'It is written,' he said to them, '"My house will be a house of prayer"; but you have made it "a den of robbers."'**
> [47]**Every day he was teaching at the temple. But the chief priests, the teachers of the law and the leaders among the people were trying to kill him.** [48]**Yet they could not find any way to do it, because all the people hung on his words.**
>
> **20:**[19]**The teachers of the law and the chief priests looked for a way**

to arrest him immediately, because they knew he had spoken this parable against them. But they were afraid of the people.

²⁰Keeping a close watch on him they sent spies, who pretended to be honest. They hoped to catch Jesus in something he said so that they might hand him over to the power and authority of the governor.

20:⁴⁵While all the people were listening, Jesus said to his disciples, ⁴⁶'Beware of the teachers of the law. They like to walk around in flowing robes and love to be greeted in the market-places and have the most important seats in the synagogues and the places of honour at banquets. ⁴⁷They devour widows' houses and for show make lengthy prayers. Such men will be punished most severely.'

21:¹One day as he was teaching the people in the temple courts and preaching the Gospel, the chief priests and the teachers of the law, together with the elders, came up to him. ²'Tell us by what authority you are doing these things', they said. 'Who gave you this authority?'

³He replied, 'I will also ask you a question. Tell me, ⁴John's baptism — was it from heaven, or from men?'

⁵They discussed it among themselves and said, 'If we say, "From heaven", he will ask, "Why didn't you believe him?" ⁶But if we say, "From men", all the people will stone us, because they are persuaded that John was a prophet.'

21:³⁷Each day Jesus was teaching at the temple, and each evening he went out to spend the night on the hill called the Mount of Olives, ³⁸and all the people came early in the morning to hear him at the temple.

22:¹Now the Feast of Unleavened Bread, called the Passover, was approaching, ²and the chief priests and the teachers of the law were looking for some way to get rid of Jesus, for they were afraid of the people. ³Then Satan entered Judas, called Iscariot, one of the Twelve. ⁴And Judas went to the chief priests and the officers of the temple guard and discussed with them how he might betray Jesus. ⁵They were delighted and agreed to give him money. ⁶He consented, and watched for an opportunity to hand Jesus over to them when no crowd was present.

22:⁴⁷While he was still speaking a crowd came up, and the man who was called Judas, one of the Twelve, was leading them. He approached Jesus to kiss him, ⁴⁸but Jesus asked him, 'Judas, are you betraying the Son of Man with a kiss?'

Jerusalem: Jesus' Salvation in Conflict with the Powerful

⁴⁹When Jesus' followers saw what was going to happen, they said, 'Lord, should we strike with our swords?' ⁵⁰And one of them struck the servant of the high priest, cutting off his right ear.

⁵¹But Jesus answered, 'No more of this!' And he touched the man's ear and healed him.

⁵²Then Jesus said to the chief priests, the officers of the temple guard, and the elders, who had come for him, 'Am I leading a rebellion, that you have come with swords and clubs? ⁵³Every day I was with you in the temple courts, and you did not lay a hand on me. But this is your hour — when darkness reigns.'

22:⁶⁶At daybreak the council of the elders of the people, both the chief priests and teachers of the law, met together, and Jesus was led before them. ⁶⁷'If you are the Christ', they said, 'tell us'.

Jesus answered, 'If I tell you, you will not believe me, ⁶⁸and if I asked you, you would not answer. ⁶⁹But from now on, the Son of Man will be seated at the right hand of the mighty God.'

⁷⁰They all asked, 'Are you then the Son of God?'

He replied, 'You are right in saying I am.'

⁷¹Then they said, 'Why do we need any more testimony? We have heard it from his own lips.'

23:¹ Then the whole assembly rose and led him off to Pilate. ²And they began to accuse him, saying, 'We have found this man subverting our nation. He opposes payments of taxes to Caesar and claims to be Christ, a king.'

³So Pilate asked Jesus, 'Are you the king of the Jews?'

'Yes, it is as you say', Jesus replied.

⁴Then Pilate announced to the chief priests and the crowd, 'I find no basis for a charge against this man.'

⁵But they insisted, 'He stirs up the people all over Judea by his teaching. He started in Galilee and has come all the way here.'

23:¹³Pilate called together the chief priests, the rulers and the people, ¹⁴and said to them, 'You brought me this man as one who was inciting the people to rebellion. I have examined him in your presence and have found no basis for your charges against him. ¹⁵Neither has Herod, for he sent him back to us; as you can see, he has done nothing to deserve death. ¹⁶Therefore, I will punish him and then release him.'

¹⁸With one voice they cried out, 'Away with this man! Release Barabbas to us!' (¹⁹Barabbas had been thrown into prison for an insurrection in the city, and for murder.)

²⁰Wanting to release Jesus, Pilate appealed to them again. ²¹But they kept shouting, 'Crucify him! Crucify him!'

²²For the third time he spoke to them: 'Why? What crime has this

man committed? I have found in him no grounds for the death penalty. Therefore I will have him punished and then release him.'

²³But with loud shouts they insistently demanded that he be crucified, and their shouts prevailed. ²⁴So Pilate decided to grant their demand. ²⁵He released the man who had been thrown into prison for insurrection and murder, the one they asked for, and surrendered Jesus to their will.

Discussion

As I said earlier, this study is going to ask the question: why, according to Luke, did the ruling class in Jerusalem want Jesus dead? The best way to answer this question might be to put ourselves in their shoes and try and see what Jesus was like from their perspective, using Luke's account of this conflict.

They had obviously heard about Jesus before he arrived in Jerusalem; his entry alone, with his singing crowd of disciples (19:37), would have alerted them to his presence, sensitive as they were to large noisy crowds. But the most remarkable thing he did, once in the city, was to go straight to the temple and create havoc by throwing out all the traders and then claiming that the temple was his house (19:45-46. In 2:49 it is 'my Father's house'.) The traders had a right to be there, after all, they had paid good money for the right to sell what the pilgrims needed; an important service to the community! And Jesus throws them out implying that they, and those who authorised their activity, are robbers.

To the chief priests, the scribes and the leaders, Jesus obviously came into Jerusalem looking for conflict. To go straight to the temple, the nerve point of Jerusalem, was hardly a diplomatic thing to do; and precisely the kind of act that would be guaranteed to raise their anger. Jesus initiated the conflict. He was the one who made the first move; and he did not let up. He settled down in the temple, invading their place of authority, and began to teach. Worst of all, the crowds loved it! (19:47-48). This threatened their authority; so they went to challenge him about whose authority he was under. He not only evaded the question but he raised the sticky problem of John the Baptist, a popular hero whom they had never liked. If they could not refute John the Baptist's authority because of their fears about his popularity with the crowd, what could they do about Jesus? This man Jesus certainly put them in a very tricky position. He undermined their authority yet they could not touch him because of his

Sydney Holo

popularity. The longer this continued the worse it would get!

And it did. Jesus told a parable in public, in their very presence, clearly implying that they were the type who not only would kill God's servants but would kill his son as well (20:9-17). He also had an encounter with some Sadducees who, hoping to discredit him in front of the crowd, came off second best. He seemed more than equal to the best of their trained academics when he met them on their own terms (20:27-40).

Jesus publicly warned his disciples about them, saying they were arrogant, hypocrites and robbers of widows. The teachers of the law, or scribes, were the lawyers of Jerusalem. It appears that Jesus accused them of defrauding widows by stealing from the estates of the deceased husbands which they controlled (20:45-47). And, said Jesus, they also mistreat the widows over the temple offerings. They have so taught and encouraged a poor widow to give to the temple that she gives everything she has and has nothing left to live on. And it is the ruling class who benefit most from the temple treasury! (21:1-4). Jesus here attacks the way the temple 'steals' from this woman. His words are a lament rather than a comment about tithing or giving alms as most commonly understood. This is a radical undermining of the interests of the ruling class. And all this is in public.

It gets worse for the controllers of the temple when Jesus makes a prediction that the temple will be destroyed. 'As for what you see here, the time will come when not one stone will be left on another; every one of them will be thrown down.' (Luke 21:6) These words must have struck a chill into the hearts of the Jerusalem authorities. This man was really and truly dangerous. What if the people believed what he said? They might forget about the temple entirely — and it looked as if the kind of Judaism he propagated was able to survive without one! All you had to do was repent and you would be saved. Something had to be done!

And the gall of the man was that he continued teaching to crowds of eager people in the temple (21:37-38). He had invaded their territory and made it his own; thrown out what he did not like, criticised the collections, and made it into his personal auditorium. His popularity with the people increased; surely in part because he was seen as a successful opponent of the elite — who were not much loved by the crowds. They undoubtedly had to silence him. He had to be put to

Jerusalem: Jesus' Salvation in Conflict with the Powerful 91

death; and only Pilate, the Roman procurator, had the authority legally to pronounce the death sentence. To put Jesus to death they had first to arrest him, and they must do this away from the crowds who loved him so much if they were to prevent a riot. Secondly, they had to get him to Pilate as soon as they could and persuade Pilate to put him to death. The crowds could do little against Pilate. The pressure was mounting for the rulers to do something before the Passover festival. Jerusalem would be crowded with tens of thousands of pilgrims; just the kind of situation this Jesus might exploit to start a disastrous riot (22:1-2).

The opportunity they had been waiting for came, quite suddenly and from an unexpected quarter: one of Jesus' very own disciples came to them and offered to guide them to Jesus when he was away from the crowds (22:1-6). The arrangements were made and Jesus was arrested outside the city, on the Mount of Olives where he had been spending the nights. Even at his arrest Jesus dominates the scene, mocking the cowardice of the rulers who have to come at night, away from the crowds, to arrest him (22:47-53). An emergency meeting of the Sanhedrin is held first thing next morning, where it is decided to take Jesus before Pilate on a multiple charge of undermining the stability of the Jewish nation, opposing the Roman taxation system, and claiming to be a king when there can be no king but Caesar (22:66-23:5). Pilate at first rejects their request that pass the death sentence, but eventually, and most reluctantly, he commands that Jesus be put to death. The upstart Galilean who had posed such a threat to the ruling class of Jerusalem was crucified, he died and was buried (23:6-55). The chief priests, the teachers of the law and the rulers of the people heaved a sigh of relief and went home to enjoy their Passover meal.

Reflection

Jesus' experience in Jerusalem is so like the experience of many who seek to bring justice in South Africa; whether in Umtata, Soweto or Cape Town.

Jesus was arrested, defenceless, by heavily armed police. They came to take him by night. They do this too in Umtata.
Judas was an informer; he was paid money to betray Jesus. This happens too in Soweto.

Jesus was interrogated and tortured in prison. They do this too in Polsmoor Prison and Victor Vester Prison.
Jesus was accused by state witnesses who deliberately bore false witness. This happens too in treason trials in Pietermaritzburg.
Jesus was sentenced to death by crucifixion. Political prisoners are hung till death in Pretoria Central Prison.

13. Jerusalem: Witness to the Risen Saviour
Luke 24:36-49; Acts 1:8; Luke 24:50-53

Luke ends his portrait of Jesus with the risen saviour appearing to his disciples, preparing them to bear witnesses to his life, death and resurrection, and then ascending into heaven leaving them with the promise that he would send the Holy Spirit to give them power to be his witnesses in all the world. Read the text reflectively, and then use this study as an opportunity to consolidate the portrait of Jesus which we have been sketching from the Gospel of Luke. If you are using this book in a group, you may like to hold a discussion on what each member has gained from these studies. Be as creative as possible in your responses; draw pictures, write Lukan confessions of faith like the one below or share stories or experiences which particularly illustrate something important you have learned.

> 24:[36]While they were still talking about this, Jesus himself stood among them and said to them, 'Peace be with you.'
> [37]They were startled and frightened, thinking they saw a ghost. [38]He said to them, 'Why are you troubled, and why do doubts rise in your minds? [39]Look at my hands and my feet. It is I myself! Touch me and see; a ghost does not have flesh and bones, as you see I have.'
> [40]When he had said this, he showed them his hands and feet. [41]And while they still did not believe it because of joy and amazement, he asked them, 'Do you have anything here to eat?' [42]They gave him a piece of broiled fish, [43]and he took it and ate it in their presence.
> [44]He said to them, 'This is what I told you while I was still with you: Everything must be fulfilled that is written about me in the Law of Moses and the Prophets and the Psalms.'

⁴⁵Then he opened their minds so they could understand the Scriptures. ⁴⁶He told them, 'This is what is written: The Christ will suffer and rise again from the dead on the third day and repentance and forgiveness of sins will be preached in his name to all nations, beginning at Jerusalem. ⁴⁸You are witnesses of these things. ⁴⁹I am going to send you what my Father has promised; but stay in the city until you have been clothed with power from on high.'

Acts 1:⁸Jesus said to them, 'But you will receive power when the Holy Spirit comes on you; and you will be my witnesses in Jerusalem, and in all Judea and Samaria, and to the ends of the earth.'

Luke 24:⁵⁰When he had led them out to the vicinity of Bethany, he lifted up his hands and blessed them. ⁵¹While he was blessing them, he left them and was taken up into heaven. ⁵²Then they worshipped him and returned to Jerusalem with great joy. ⁵³And they stayed continually at the temple, praising God.

Discussion

Several points emerge in these readings which we must notice for Luke's portrait of Jesus. Firstly, Luke is emphatic that Jesus rose from the dead (24:36-43). Luke records two previous resurrection appearances: to the women at the tomb (24:1-8) and to the men on the road to Emmaus (24:13-35). In the third resurrection appearance the emphasis is on the physical body of the resurrected Jesus. The disciples can see and touch Jesus; and he eats before them. This is no ghost or spirit, but the risen Jesus. For Luke's readers this was critical; Christianity could only survive if Jesus had in fact risen from the dead. If not, the central confession of faith of the early Church was undermined.

Secondly, (24:44-49; Acts 1:8) Jesus promises to send the disciples the Holy Spirit which will fill them with power to be witnesses to the salvation Jesus has brought. Forgiveness of sins will be preached to the whole world. Jesus is the saviour of the world, for his disciples will carry the message from Jerusalem to the ends of the earth. And this will be done, typically for Luke, in the power of the Holy Spirit.

Thirdly, Jesus ascends to heaven. Jesus' Galilean ministry culminated in him going up the mountain and being transfigured alongside Moses and Elijah. At the culmination of his work in the city of destiny he goes up to heaven as Elijah did; taken up by God. He leaves the disciples and they return to Jerusalem to await their destiny. Just as the birth of Jesus is inextricably linked to the Holy Spirit and Jerusalem, so too is the birth of the Church tied to Jerusalem and the Holy Spirit. It is in this city of destiny that the Holy Spirit will come upon them and it is in this city of destiny that the Church will first bear witness to Jesus, the Saviour of the World.

Reflection: a Lukan Confession of Faith

We confess the gospel by which we are saved. Christ suffered, he was crucified and buried, and on the third day he rose from the dead.
We believe in Jesus Christ:
whose way was prepared by the son of a barren woman,
who was born to an unmarried mother,
whose coming into this world was shrouded by the Holy Spirit.
We believe in Jesus Christ who was sent out into the world in the power of the Holy Spirit and defeated the devil in the wilderness, cast out demons, taught with authority and brought people to the salvation of God.
We believe in the saviour whose salvation was too costly for the rich ruler but was welcomed by the despised Zacchaeus; the saviour, the friend of tax collectors and sinners.
We believe in Jesus Christ whose destiny lay in Jerusalem, where his angry conflict with the tyrant rulers of the city lead to his death.
We believe in a human saviour who sweated drops like blood as he faced crucifixion and who died for the forgiveness of sins.
We believe in the divine saviour who rose on the third day and sent his disciples into the world in the power of the Holy Spirit.

Prayer

Send us out into the world
in the power of the Holy Spirit
that we may be witnesses to your salvation in our Jerusalem
and to the ends of the earth.
Amen

A SCHOLARLY NOTE

Throughout my work the magisterial commentary on Luke by Joseph A. Fitzmyer, *The Gospel to According to Luke* Vol 1 & 2, (New York: Doubleday, 1981 & 1985), has proved invaluable. The other major commentary I used is I.Howard Marshall, *The Gospel of Luke: A Commentary on the Greek Text* (Exeter: Paternoster, 1978.) The academic literature on the Gospel of Luke is vast. The work of Helmut Conzelmann, *The Theology of St Luke* (London: Faber & Faber, 1960), remains foundational and underlies most modern scholarship on Luke. Much of the most recent literature has stressed the socio-political dimensions of Jesus' life and the Gospel narratives, see especially the works cited in suggested reading. The literature on the background to Jesus is even more vast. Here are the works which I have found to be particularly useful in this regard: Sean Freyne, *Galilee from Alexander the Great to Hadrian: 323 BCE-135 CE* (Delaware: Michael Glazier, 1980); Richard A. Horsley and John S. Hanson, *Bandits, Prophets and Messiahs* (New York: Winston Press, 1985); Shaye J.D. Cohen, *From Maccabees to the Mishnah* (Philadelphia: Westminster, 1987); the volume edited by Norman K. Gottwald, *The Bible and Liberation* (Maryknoll, NY: Orbis, 1983), has a number of useful articles, but some of the material in the book is dated. The initial chapters of Fernando Belo, *A Materialist Reading of the Gospel of Mark* (Maryknoll, NY: Orbis, 1974) are still very useful. Emil Schurer's *The History of the Jewish People in the Age of Jesus Christ* Vol 1,2, & 3i,ii (Edinburgh: T & T Clark, 1971-1987), in its new revision remains the classic text; as does Helmut Koester's *Introduction to the New Testament* (Berlin: De Gruyter, 1982).

SUGGESTED READINGS

Many of the best books written on the Gospels are far too scholarly to be read by a wide audience. Two of the less academically demanding books which I recommend are Michel Clevenot, *Materialist Approaches to the Bible* (Maryknoll, NY: Orbis, 1985), the second part of which is devoted to the Gospel of Mark, and Hugo Echegaray, *The Practice of Jesus* (Maryknoll, NY: Orbis, 1984). The best on Luke is Luise Schrottoff and Wolfgang Stegemann, *Jesus and the Hope of the Poor* (Maryknoll, NY: Orbis, 1986). Other works which focus on socio-political aspects of Luke are Richard J. Cassidy, *Jesus, Politics and Society* (Maryknoll, NY: Orbis, 1978); Richard J. Cassidy and Philip J. Scharper (eds), *Political Issues in Luke-Acts* (Maryknoll, NY: Orbis, 1983) and J. Massyngbaerde Ford, *My Enemy is My Guest: Jesus and Violence in Luke* (Maryknoll, NY: Orbis, 1984.)